ERASING REASON

*Inside Aesthetic Realism – A Cult That Tried to
Turn Queer People Straight*

Hal W. Lanse, PhD

Introduction by Michael Bluejay

This book is not intended to dispense medical or psychological treatment. If you have been victimized by a cult and feel you need help for this or any other reason, seek the attention of a medical or mental health professional immediately.

All names have been changed except for the following individuals: Eli Siegel, his wife, Martha Baird Siegel, Ellen Reiss, the current cult leader, Timothy Lynch, a teacher in the AR cult and Reiss' husband, and Arnold Perey, AR's spokesman and a leader in the cult.

Michael Bluejay, a former AR member who was raised in the cult, has placed himself on the record as a public critic of AR. His website (http://michaelbluejay.com/x/) exposes the cult's practices. Michael is a major contributor to this book.

The author of this book, Hal W. Lanse, PhD, also an AR survivor, uses his real name. Gladly.

A note on language: The author of this book prefers to use the controversial word "queer" as opposed to the more commonly used "gay." "Queer" is interpreted by some (including the author) to mean "a deviation from the norm." Deviation, however, is not viewed by this author as negative. Just different. "Gay" cuts too close to the author's unhappy memories of terms like "light in the loafers," "fairy," "limp-wristed," and "pansy." "Invert" is too antediluvian and "Sodomite" reeks of blame. So "queer" is the word of choice in this book. Some (though certainly not all) members of the LGBT community are uncomfortable with the word. To those with demurs: We'll have to agree to disagree on this issue.

Michael Bluejay, in his introduction, prefers the more widely used: "gay."

CONTENTS

Everybody's journey is individual. If you fall in love with a boy, you fall in love with a boy. The fact that many Americans consider it a disease says more about them than it does about homosexuality.

-James Baldwin

INTRODUCTION

When I was twelve years old, I stood silently in front of the New York Times building with other members of a cult called Aesthetic Realism (AR), to protest the Times' "refusal" to write about AR, especially about AR's "gay cure." It wasn't the first time I'd protested against the Times. My family had me holding AR signs at the NYT building at least as early as age three. My parents were followers of Aesthetic Realism. I was born into this mind-control cult. I was considered "lucky" by other followers to have had a personal "lesson" with the founder and leader, Eli Siegel when I was two-years-old. My mother was born into the group too, because her parents were AR devotees.

Exactly what is a mind-control cult? In my experience as an anti-cult activist, most people don't really know. The popular idea is that a cult is a group with weird beliefs about UFOs or the end of the world or other strange matters. These are the sensationalistic things that make the news. But some cults' beliefs can appear entirely reasonable, even laudable.

What makes a cult a cult is not what they believe, but the fanatical devotion to those beliefs, along with the psychological manipulation of the members that goes along with it. Aesthetic Realism isn't a cult because its members believe that "contempt for the world" poisons the soul (one of their core beliefs). AR is a cult because its members believe that the man who built a philosophy around that idea was the greatest human being who ever lived, and that the AR philosophy is the single-most important thing in the world. AR is a cult because its leaders employ mind-control methods to get its members to adopt and keep those beliefs.

So how do people get sucked into cults in the first place? The general public often thinks that cult followers are "stupid," but that's just not true. The fact is most of us are vulnerable to psychological manipulation, no matter how smart we are. Decades of scientific research have shown as much. A former member of a different cult writes (*International Cultic Studies Newsletter*, Vol. 4, No. 1, February 2005):

After leaving my former group, I was so convinced that I had to be intellectually deficient that I actually took an I.Q. test. Much to my surprise, instead of scoring way below average, I scored in the 97th percentile. As I have learned more about the kinds of people cults recruit, I have found that I am the rule and not the exception. Because the rigors of cult life are arduous, these groups do not want someone who will break down easily. Cults go after the best and the brightest—robbing all of us of people who could be making a huge difference in this world.

Science can help us understand why people fall-in with cults. A peek at the research is scary. As an example, in the 1950s Solomon Asch conducted experiments in which subjects were asked to identify which of three lines on a card was the same length as the sole line on another card. In each case, three people were shown the cards and gave answers. What the subject didn't know is that the other two people giving answers were confederates (fake subjects). They'd begin normally, but then the confederates would start offering answers that were clearly wrong. What did the subjects do when they saw these wrong answers? In many cases the subjects would give the same wrong answer in order to be in step with the confederates. In fact, a whopping seventy-five percent of the subjects gave at least one clearly-wrong answer in order to match the confederates' answers.

 This experiment demonstrates powerfully people's need to conform, and how we often make decisions for social-emotional reasons rather than obeying the precepts of strict logic. When I tell people about this experiment, they invariably believe that they would fall into the twenty-five percent group that never gave a wrong answer.

In another set of experiments conducted by Stanley Milgram, the researcher instructed the subject (the "teacher") to press a button to give an electric shock to another subject (the "student") whenever the student gave the wrong answer to a question. What the teacher didn't know was that the student was actually a confederate and wasn't really getting shocked.

As the test progressed, the student would continue to give wrong answers and the researcher would instruct the teacher to deliver increasingly painful shocks to the student. The student would cry out in (fake) pain, begging for the test to end; but the researcher told the teacher that he must continue. Here again, sixty-five percent of the teachers went through the whole test, administering the final shock of what they thought was four-hundred-fifty volts! When I tell people about this, they're confident that they would be among the thirty-five percent who refused to give the final shock.

Other experiments revealed the power of cognitive dissonance, which in layman's terms is the tendency to choose the conclusion that's more comfortable rather than the one that's more reasonable. For example, if someone presents a cult member with arguments or evidence that they're in a cult, the cult member will have to make a choice: Am I really in a cult, which means that I embarrassingly had the wool pulled over my eyes, and I've wasted all my time on something fraudulent? Or is my group legitimate, holding the one true answer to everything in the world? Guess which choice people will make most of the time?

Powerful psychological forces affect us all the time, even if we're smarter than average. As Scott Adams said, "The fascinating thing about cognitive dissonance is that it's immune to intelligence. No matter how smart you are, you can't think your way out of it. Once your actions and your self-image get out of sync, the result is an absurd rationalization."

Imagine how effective a cult that knows these tricks can be when it deliberately uses them to exploit and manipulate its members. That's mind control.

Here's the standard recipe for controlling someone's mind:

- Shower a potential recruit with lots of attention and praise. Cult experts call this "love bombing." That's enough to get a recruit's attention, but it's not enough to get them indoctrinated. More steps are needed.

- Tell the recruit that the group has the secret answer to the meaning of life, or the one true knowledge of the world, or the solution to some problem the recruit has such as alcoholism, depression, stuttering or, in the case of Aesthetic Realism, being gay. Whatever the carrot is, dangle the carrot in front of the inductee.

- Induce guilt. Cults have a process in which the inductee is criticized in order to make him or her feel small. This makes the individual a lot more vulnerable to having new ideas implanted by cult leaders. The inductee may resist this process, but the leaders are ready for that: they just dangle the carrot some more. ("If you want to stop being gay, then you'll have to understand the contempt you have for others and you'll have to express total, unreserved gratitude for what we're teaching you.") You can see this clearly in the transcript of an AR therapy session (called a "consultation") sent to me by an AR survivor after he left the group. It is reproduced as an appendix to this book.

Once followers are inducted, cognitive dissonance keeps them in. It's uncomfortable for converts to conclude that they made a mistake by joining. It takes a long time to come to such a conclusion. Some followers never wake up.

Hal Lanse woke up. An AR survivor, Lanse tells his story and provides an in-depth look at mind control and AR's specific uses of mind-control techniques.

From the sixties through the eighties, Aesthetic Realism actively promoted its gay cure. Shortly after I launched my website exposing the cult, the Aesthetic Realists struck back with their own website, accusing me of lying about this issue. They say:

Michael Bluejay writes: "AR says that homosexuality is a mental illness" and "AR professed to have the "cure" for homosexuality." This is completely untrue...Aesthetic Realism never saw homosexuality as something to "cure," and...never presented itself as having a "cure."

Is that so? The evidence says otherwise:

- The Aesthetic Realists published two different books on the subject: The H Persuasion: How Persons Have Permanently Changed From Homosexuality through the Study of Aesthetic Realism with Eli Siegel and The Aesthetic Realism of Eli Siegel and the Change from Homosexuality.

- They made a film about their program called *Yes, We Have Changed* [from homosexuality].

- They did various television interviews to promote their "cure," including two appearances on the David Susskind Show.

- They bought advertising space boasting of the gay cure in the *New York Times*, *The Los Angeles Times* and *The Washington Post*. The ad says: "We say what history will say: the American press has blood on its hands, has caused misery and death, because for years it has withheld the news that men and women have changed from homosexuality through study of Aesthetic Realism."

- They conducted an inquest of an AR disciple (supposedly cured of his gayness and quickly married off to a female follower) when he was found to still be cruising for gay sex. The follower was harassed and drummed out of the cult in an attempt to hide AR's failure to alter his homosexuality. A transcript of that meeting first appeared on my website. It appears as an appendix to this book.

Here's a telling quote from the preface of one of AR's books. It is written by Ellen Reiss, the current leader (called "class chairman") of the cult: "It is a beautiful fact that through study of Aesthetic

Realism, the philosophy founded by the American poet and critic Eli Siegel, men have changed from homosexuality...Eli Siegel's statement of the cause of homosexuality [contempt for the world and women]...is scientific law."

In light of such voluminous evidence, how can AR followers justify their claim that they never promoted a gay cure? The answer is they simply never used the word "cure" themselves. It's like a racist website I once visited. In their FAQs, they said something like this:

Q: Are you racist?

A: No! We just believe all races should be segregated for the purpose of ethnic purity. But we're not racists or anything.

The Aesthetic Realists play the same game:

Q: Did you ever claim to have a cure for homosexuality?

A: No, and anyone who says we did is a liar! We just ran a program to show gay people that their homosexuality is unethical, selfish and a product of their contempt for the world. We merely explained that by realizing the truth they'd cease to be gay. But we never said we had a gay cure or anything.

AR didn't start out as an anti-gay group and changing gays wasn't its focus for a long time. But in the late 1960s the group and its leader, Eli Siegel, realized they could get publicity for their purported ability to turn gays straight. So they milked the idea for all it was worth. But really, their goal wasn't to "fix" all the gays in the world. Rather, the gay cure was just a way to get people interested in Aesthetic Realism. Their real goal, then and now, was to get the world to adopt AR's doctrines and to believe that AR is the most important thing in the world: the one and only beautiful truth. Fixing gays was just a means to that end.

By 1990, the Aesthetic Realists were forced to abandon their gay therapy program. Society was getting a lot more tolerant and their efforts to reform gays made the AR Foundation stick out like a sore thumb in a neighborhood that has a large, openly gay population. Equally important: Most of AR's supposed success stories fell off the wagon and reverted to a gay life. That was mighty embarrassing for the Aesthetic Realists the few times the press ever did come calling, asking to interview the people in AR's books and advertisements. Oops!

AR is still anti-gay. They've never admitted that their program to change gays was wrong. They haven't recanted, and they've certainly never apologized for it. They still believe that homosexuality is a mental condition caused by contempt for the world. They still believe that by studying Aesthetic Realism one can learn to like the world properly and thus stop being gay. They have to believe this because their founder and leader said it was so. No cult ever goes against the teachings of its leader.

I was raised inside Aesthetic Realism, but I eventually got out. My mother's marriage to another Aesthetic Realist ended early-on. When I was young, my mother met another man who loved her but saw that she had become a cult zombie and that I was about to become one, too. He married her and took us to Texas to get us away from the cult. (After seventy years in business, AR hasn't managed to spread outside of SoHo in New York City; so Texas was certainly a safe-haven.)

When I was a teenager, my mother suddenly snapped out of it. That was fine with me. I had never really cared for AR. As I got older I finally understood that Aesthetic Realism was actually a mind-control group. I decided to launch a website to show the world what Aesthetic Realism really is.

Hal Lanse, a survivor of AR's gay cure, came to a similar decision. He began by publishing a statement about his AR experiences on the website called I'm from Driftwood. That article is included in this book. Now, Dr. Hal (as he is often called) has written this extensive book on AR's cult activities and homophobic practices.

Dr. Hal has done a great service by pulling back the curtain on Aesthetic Realism and showing how the group hurts people. I'm happy that he has joined me in my cult-busting efforts.

-Michael Bluejay, 2012

Forward

Why This Book?

Culturally, the world is changing. More queer people can live openly in this and many other industrialized nations. There's less in the way of prejudice. Less to hide from. Less to fear. But that doesn't mean there's nothing to fear. Queer people are victimized every day. Just look at the FBI's most recent statistics. In 2010 (the Bureau's most recently published data) there were 1,470 violent crimes against LGBT people reported. (Remember, these are just the crimes that were *reported*.) The FBI's statistics cite (among other hate crimes):

- 247 acts of aggravated assault

- 495 acts of simple assault

- 331 acts of intimidation

The number of psychological assaults would be hard to calculate. Many victims are afraid to come forward. And then there are the public assaults that do inestimable damage: politicians who repudiate gay marriage, preachers who malign queer people from the pulpit, the widespread use of terms like "homo" and "faggot" and "that's so gay." All of the words, insults, dismissals and contempt that the LGBT community lives with every day does harm to the hearts and minds of individuals whose only "crime" is that they were born into a sexual minority.

When individuals, groups, and homophobic cults try to alter people's sexuality, whether they call it a cure or simply a "change," they are in fact assaulting those individuals. They are attacking queer folks' self-esteem and this can lead to a host of social and emotional troubles.

One way to defend queer people is to speak about the injustices against them. That is the purpose of this book. The focus will be on one particular cult: The Aesthetic Realism of Eli Siegel. This small but insidious cult began in the 1940s. In its early days, one member claimed to have converted from queer to straight. But the cult really picked up steam in the 60s, 70s and 80s when it received some media coverage for its claim to have "changed" queer men into straight ones. That's when the author of this book joined (and later escaped).

In the 60s through the 80s, conversion efforts were a major focus of AR and its publicity machine. The talk shows on which followers appeared centered on the so-called "change from homosexuality." Monthly seminars and weekly pseudo-therapy sessions focused on queer conversion efforts.

Erasing Reason is written by a survivor of Aesthetic Realism. The author's story, first published on the website *I'm from Driftwood* (www.imfromdriftwood.com) is re-issued at the end of this book (Appendix One).

This exposé will demonstrate, first of all, why Aesthetic Realism can be fairly called a cult. It will examine the group's *modus operandi,* its internal culture and its philosophical underpinnings. You will learn, too, why AR must be viewed as junk science, not genuine science. It is absent of any legitimate scientific research. You will learn about the harm that this and similar groups can and have done. Why do so many health organizations repudiate reparative therapy and any similar approaches? Read and learn!

One might ask, is AR an "ex-gay" cult? No, that's a term that refers specifically to certain Christian cults. AR is not a Christian cult. It is homophobic but not, strictly speaking, an "ex-gay" group.

Aesthetic Realism and its founder Eli Siegel are purveyors of anti-queer prejudice. Siegel's legacy is one of great damage and great insult to the LGBT community. (In one of his lectures he actually mocked homosexuals by affecting a lisp.)

One front in the battle for civil rights is the historical front: the documentation of homophobia and its past and present impact on the queer community. Constructing an understanding of the past and present techniques of homophobia can prevent individuals from future victimhood. The author believes that building such an understanding can help people comprehend and hopefully mitigate the impact of all sorts of cults, not just homophobic ones.

At the very least, queer voices can force bigots to walk on eggshells as Aesthetic Realism devotees now do. AR no longer gives public presentations on the "change from homosexuality." But they haven't repudiated their cult's homophobic beliefs. Some years back they put out this statement:

It is a fact that men and women have changed from homosexuality through the study of Aesthetic Realism. Meanwhile, as is well known, there is now intense anger in America on the subject of homosexuality and how it is seen. Since this subject is by no means central to Aesthetic Realism, and since the Aesthetic Realism Foundation has not wanted to be involved in that atmosphere of anger, in 1990 the Foundation discontinued its public presentation of the fact that through Aesthetic Realism people have changed from homosexuality, and consultations to change from homosexuality are not being given. That is because we do not want this matter, which is certainly not fundamental to Aesthetic Realism, to be used to obscure what Aesthetic Realism truly is: education of the largest, most cultural kind.

They haven't backed down from their homophobic beliefs. And in the absence of any authentic research the AR Foundation cannot, in all fairness, claim that it is a "fact" that queer people have gone straight. These days, the AR Foundation simply won't open their doors to public scrutiny. They've been taken to task publicly for their homophobic practices. There have even been demonstrations at their doorstep. So they simply won't expose themselves to public censure anymore. They've drawn a curtain on their collective bigotry.

It's ironic: AR often demands that the rest of the world be "completely fair" to their progenitor and his teachings. But they also keep Siegel's homophobic ravings under wraps. They want fairness (really lionization) to run concurrently with public blindness.

Unfortunately for the AR censors, books and other documents have been published over the years and AR's views on homosexuality are well-documented. These documents are easy to track down. Additionally, former disciples are more than happy to share their experiences. Many of their contributions are included here. Many more are included on Michael Bluejay's anti-cult website: http://michaelbluejay.com/x/.

The purpose of this book is to shine a light into the dark corners of Aesthetic Realism, to expose the group's essential homophobia and to demonstrate the cult's shocking treatment of those who come under its sway. The author believes that by turning on the torch he is indeed being (in the cultists' own words) "completely fair" to Eli Siegel, his teachings and his disciples' practices. This book serves as a cautionary tale about the threat of aggressive homophobia and the insidious impact of cult participation.

One

Thought Reform

Cults are destructive, but they're also organized, fanatical and very skilled at warping members' thought processes. There's a dark talent that cult leaders develop. Cults get into their followers' heads and retard their critical thinking skills. Rick Ross's anti-cult website (www.rickross.com) describes the techniques by which this mind warping is done. An article on the site, written by John Stacey, summarizes the work of Robert Jay Lifton and other cult experts. How do cults attract and control followers? The process is called thought reform: a pretty euphemism for an ugly set of psychological attacks.

Milieu Control

Aesthetic Realists use all of the identified thought reform techniques. *Milieu control* is one subcategory. Stacey tells us that "speaking or acting in ways that are in conflict with the group members who dominate the environment makes a [potential member] feel awkward and wrong—though he may be acting in an acceptable manner according to societal norms."

Aesthetic Realists don't just tell new and potential members that they must behave in a certain manner (though this certainly goes on in spades). When you're in an environment where everyone acts in certain ways you learn to emulate such behavior in order to fit in. AR provides a good deal of such behavioral modeling.

For example, when one follower complained that she didn't always want to go to the AR Foundation on Saturday nights but wanted to go sometimes to the movies, a leader raised her hand and said: "You have a right to go wherever you want. Personally, there's no other place in the world I'd rather be on a Saturday night than the Aesthetic Realism Foundation."

See? The individual wasn't told "no" but she was publicly shamed by another member who demonstrated a higher level of commitment.

Aesthetic Realists praise and extol those who embrace their internal norms. Wearing Victim of the Press buttons was one such norm. You wore one because everyone did. This practice went on for years so that AR followers could proclaim their perceived sense of victimization every day. Siegel ordered followers to wear them. He claimed he wasn't famous because the media was "boycotting" him and his work. The buttons were a way of demonstrating solidarity with Siegel's perceived victimhood.

The Victim of the Press buttons also provided a means of advertising the group when out in public. For years, disciples wore the buttons on the streets, at work (compromising their jobs), at meetings and even, in some cases, on their pajamas. They grew fanatical about wearing the button at all times and in all places. Brides wore them on their wedding gowns. They were placed on children's clothing.

Another behavioral norm: You are expected to send gratitude letters to group leaders (and in his lifetime to Siegel himself) because it is a way of showing that you've gotten with the program. People host "gratitude parties," get-togethers where followers serve heroes and spend the day offering testimonials and applauding one another for compliance with internal norms.

You are praised for praising. One former member says: "If a couple already had a solid marriage or if a teacher was already successful in the classroom... (Both things Aesthetic Realists refused to acknowledge could exist outside of AR), they were discouraged from speaking about that. Instead, we all had to present ourselves as essentially miserable failures whose lives were in shambles until we found the glorious "answers to all our questions" in AR. If members were accused of being ungrateful for what AR had done for them, they might be told to "have a courageous memory" and recall how awful life had been before AR."

If you stick around long enough and frequently praise AR and its leaders you are lauded for being "steady." This means you're a consistent supporter. You are a "friend" to Aesthetic Realism, as opposed to the media and former members who are "enemies" of the group. These words are actually used by AR followers. Often.

Friends? Enemies? It all seems very junior high to people on the outside; but members of cults are very concerned with who likes them and who does not. AR, like any good cult, loves its cheerleaders and abhors its detractors.

AR even gets into adherents' bedrooms. Literally. One former follower, contributing to Michael Bluejay's online exposé of AR, tells us: "Even when in the grip of passion, one was supposed to be impelled to express gratitude to Siegel, AR and [current leader] Reiss for making the union possible. If one did not feel that impulsion, it meant they were misusing sex."

Oral sex and masturbation, even in the heterosexual arena, were considered emanations of contempt. Anything that fell outside the arena of missionary-style heterosexual coupling was strictly verboten.

Mystical Manipulation

Another element of thought reform is called *mystical manipulation*. John Stacey tells us that this is a way of rewarding followers by having them feel like they are "God's elect"—superior to all others. AR leaders frequently praise members by telling them that they have "seen the truth of Aesthetic Realism" and that they will be "teaching the world" someday. [Reality check: They've been around since the 1940s and they're still not teaching the world.]

Aesthetic Realists are encouraged by their leaders to see themselves as the vanguard of a new world. Every cult uses this selling point in one form or another and AR hasn't missed its opportunity here. People who leave are thought to have betrayed the cult and the world itself. One member went so far as to say to a class of AR leaders that in the new world AR deserters should be rounded up and executed. No one in the room challenged this statement.

Sexual Purity

A common form of thought reform is the demand for *sexual purity*. Cult members, Stacey tells us, are "...expected to become celibate until the group approved of a sanctioned sexual relationship." Aesthetic Realists, especially those high up on the ladder, are expected to couple within the group. This isn't always an explicit demand. But the pressure is there.

It is the norm for upper-echelon members to marry within the group. If your spouse leaves the cult and you divorce, it is expected that you will couple with yet another insider. Lower echelon adherents (consultees) are sometimes fed suggestions for possible mates. Queer ("changed") followers, especially, are pressured to mate outside their gender but within the group. And so we come to the ultimate demand for sexual purity: the demand to go straight, or in AR parlance to "change" from homosexuality.

Mind you, no one forces queer people to undergo this process. But AR did much of its homophobic work in the 70s and 80s, when the Gay Liberation Movement was just getting started. Society, for the most part, viewed homosexuality as a perversion, a sin and a sickness.

A brave minority of queer people came out of the closet and fought back during that era. But many queers held to the silent majority. They were closeted, frightened and shame-based. Even today there are plenty of homosexuals who internalize society's negative stereotypes of LGBT people. This is why conversion groups still get traction.

Siegel began his homophobic work in the 40s, when he roped-in his first self-hater. But when some of his followers went on television in the 70s and again in the 80s to proclaim that they had "changed from homosexuality" Siegel's "fifteen minutes of fame" began.

Followers began pestering the *New York Times* and other media outlets for coverage. They gave consultations (pseudo-therapy sessions) to self-haters who hoped to go straight. They even spent members' money to buy an ad in the *New York Times* proclaiming "We Have Changed from Homosexuality." You can see the ad in

26

Appendix Two. This author's name was included—a claim that is herein retracted.

So how did AR's particular brand of sexual purity manifest? Siegel summed it up as follows: "All homosexuality arises from contempt of the world; not liking it sufficiently. This changes to contempt for women."

Michael Bluejay's website refers to AR's attempt to "cure" homosexuality. The AR folks claim that they never tried to cure homosexuality. They deny that they've given therapy. But they also contradict themselves. In the *New York Daily News* (March 15th, 1981), AR's current leader, Ellen Reiss, is quoted as saying: "We are not psychiatrists; psychiatry has essentially failed. People who go to psychiatrists don't change. They don't get better...if a [homosexual] person wants to change we offer them a scientific, logical approach."

Clearly, AR has positioned itself publicly as the alternative to psychiatry. And despite AR's insistence that the cult never tried to "cure" homosexuals, Reiss claims that through AR homosexuals can "get better." It sure sounds like a cure.

Reiss offers no scientific evidence that AR's approach is more effective than any of the many therapeutic modalities that were available at the time the News article was published. If she's capable of distinguishing between science and medical mythology it's not on display in the *Daily News*.

Historian Martin Duberman's memoir *Cures: A Gay Man's Odyssey* casts further doubt upon AR's claim that they never tried to cure queer people. In 1972, Duberman came out of the closet in a New York Times article. He received many letters after the article was published and reports that: "Several devotees of Aesthetic Realism—Eli Siegel's "philosophy of living"—assured me that their group had had great success in converting homosexuals and suggested I present myself for cure."

AR's position as to the ethics (or lack thereof as they see it) of homosexuals goes further than calling queer people merely diseased. It is an ethical failing beginning in early childhood, Siegel insisted. His so-called Aesthetic Realism lessons and the consultations given by his self-hating proselytizers consisted of criticizing queer followers' "contempt for the world" and uncovering the "narrow selves" they supposedly developed as little children.

The demand for purity, John Stacey says, leads to a loss of self-esteem. When you criticize a person's world view, his or her relationships, sexual proclivities, even the way he or she speaks (people are often lambasted for a perceived unacceptable tone of voice in AR) then the psychological ground you walk on is shaky at best. AR adherents claim that they only tried to help people who "wanted" to change. Playing into someone's self-doubts, however, is neither a legitimate nor an ethical way to help them.

AR disciples take their brand of sexual purity quite far. In the early 80s, one Aesthetic Realism leader posited that AIDS might be caused by contempt for the world that runs so deep in homosexual men it alters the "germ-plasm." [His words.] Other insiders agreed that this was a reasonable theory. In other words, AR leaders blamed the disease on its victims.

Then, there was the case of Aaron Bauer an HIV positive man. "The ARists were terrified of AIDS," a former insider writes. "There was one consultee, Aaron Bauer who was HIV positive and wanted to continue consultations to discuss how to handle having this illness. The leaders were between a rock and a hard place because they didn't want any "infected" people anywhere near the Aesthetic Realism Foundation. But they knew it would look bad if they forbade him from having any more consultations. So the arrangement was that Aaron couldn't come to public programs or set foot inside the AR Foundation except for consultations; and while there, he wasn't to use the men's room or touch anything. He was to come, have the consultation and leave immediately."

Aesthetic Realism's obsession over purity makes its followers frightened and cruel. The ex-insider who shared this story adds, "I also remember that a nurse who was an AR consultee regularly visited Aaron in the hospital when he was nearing the end. She had been very good friends with him and didn't want to abandon him in his greatest time of need. Instead of respecting her as I think they should have, the AR leaders were really disgusted with her for this. However, they knew better than to tell her their feelings because of how it would look. They thought she should have known on her own to stay far away from Aaron Bauer out of loyalty to Aesthetic Realism because she was one of the few people alive who possessed the most precious knowledge in the world (AR). In endangering her life (as they saw it), the leaders believed that the nurse was being careless with this great knowledge."

Clearly, AR's leaders felt that Aaron would compromise their purity and that of other devotees. Aaron Bauer was treated like a leper. If left to the leadership, no one from AR would have visited and comforted him in his final days.

The Cult of Confession

Cults gather intimate, highly-personal information about their members. Confessions are used to bolster (at least in the eyes of adherents) the public reputation of the cult. Says John Stacey: "Cults use this knowledge, found through personal confessions, as proof that the newcomer's life before the cult was corrupt and repugnant—compared to the correct way of living as prescribed by the group." Additionally, reformation through the cult often goes hand-in-hand with miraculous life-transformations.

Do AR devotees follow this pattern? Decide for yourself. All of the quotes below have been published online or in AR's books The H Persuasion and The Aesthetic Realism of Eli Siegel and the Change from Homosexuality. All of the online quotes were available on the Internet on the day this book was published. The author reached out to the individuals quoted and to the AR Foundation in case anyone wished to retract or modify their statements. None of them indicated that they wished to do so.

These statements include confessions about men's unhappy homosexual lives as well as a host of other confessions:

"The very fact that I can *speak* on the subject of expressing oneself, I owe to Eli Siegel, the great American poet, critic and founder of the education Aesthetic Realism. As a person who stuttered painfully from the time I was three years old, my ability to express myself was very much hindered before I began to study Aesthetic Realism."

"Studying how the world we are meeting all the time is a oneness of opposites...I felt I had new eyes as I began seeing beauty that my conceit had obscured."

"The truth was, I went from being for a man to being against him very fast, and my relationships did not fare well. I assumed it was the men's fault...I'm grateful Eli Siegel enabled me to make sense of how I was for and against [my boyfriend]."

"I had based my personality on quietly sneering at the world and people; including my parents, teachers and men...I loathed myself..."

"I am very grateful to Aesthetic Realism and its founder, Eli Siegel for understanding the cause of eating disorders...the ten-year hell I was in [ended] completely."

"Once, I was a cold snob who contemptuously dismissed most of humanity, beginning with my father, as beneath me."

"I once felt like a terrific coward because of my fears, which I was once ashamed to speak of. I was afraid to stay home alone and afraid to leave my home."

"I deeply regret that I once [in childhood] called a little boy an ugly [racial] name...The memory of his pained face fills me with shame even after all these years. I don't know how my life would have gone if my parents had not begun to study Aesthetic Realism."

"I looked squarely at how ugly, how prejudiced my thoughts had been, how steep my contempt was for the Arab people, seeing them as less human than we Israelis were."

"I never felt good before, during and after [queer sex], though I was propelled and compelled...I constantly was saying, 'Maybe if I hate it enough I won't do it again.'"

[Ed.: The same individual made the following attack on other queer people.]

"...there's a kind of flamboyant homosexuality. If you watch them, just in terms of behavior, so clearly there is contempt."

"I had tried to make homosexuality work, but each year I was growing colder and further away from myself and people...I thought of suicide quite a bit."

"There was a discomfort with it [homosexuality] because I couldn't respect the pleasure I was having...when I have my arms around my wife...I feel the pleasure of respect...she stands for a world I can like more." [Ed.: The couple divorced.]

On the David Susskind Show of May 8th, 1989: "Mr. Siegel, I'm thirty-four years old. For the first time in my life I've had sex with a woman, and the feeling, I can't describe it, it's so different from what I felt in homosexuality...as I was close to a man, afterwards there would be a tremendous sense of repulsion..."

A follower was asked by Siegel: "...were you at ease [with being queer]? "I seemed to be." "I think you were uneasy, guilty and bored."

[Ed.: This last quote is typical of Siegel's method. He would often tell people what they thought or should think. Shame-based people will often find themselves agreeing with the opinions of an authority figure.]

David Susskind: [Same episode as above] "Are you suggesting that any practicing homosexual...has a negative view of the world and himself, and is probably consciously or unconsciously desirous of changing?" The Aesthetic Realists' collect response: "Yes, definitely."

Sacred Science

Before discussing the nature of *sacred science* and AR's use of this classic cult technique, we must ask another question. What is the real thing? What is science?

One answer is that science is a concerted attempt to prove a theory wrong. If, after exhaustive efforts, the theory cannot be disproven, then science can make a reasonable assumption that the theory is valid. Real science always holds the assumption that new data can come-in rendering a previously supported theory invalid.

The word *truth* (a word that is popular in AR circles) never comes into the mix. When one talks of truth, science has been abandoned in favor of faith. The objection here is that the late

Siegel and his disciples have asserted that Aesthetic Realism is scientific. There is absolutely no science in the Aesthetic Realism of Eli Siegel.

Real scientists proceed as follows:

- They propose a question.

- They research the topic by reading and analyzing everything written on the topic in peer reviewed journals (scientific periodicals where research is vetted by established scientists in the field).

- They construct a hypothesis (theory).

- They systematically test the hypothesis.

- They report their results in a peer reviewed journal so that established experts in the field can critique the researcher's methodologies and conclusions.

One significant methodology is the *randomized controlled study*. In this type of research, "...subjects...are randomly allocated to receive one or other of the alternative treatments under study... two (or more) groups of subjects are followed in exactly the same way, and the only differences between the care they receive...should be those intrinsic to the treatments being compared." (*Wikipedia*)

There are no randomized controlled studies of Siegel's theories about homosexuality. Neither Siegel nor any of his supporters have published research in peer reviewed journals on the subject of homosexuality or on any other subject. Their assertions about the "change from homosexuality" are based on anecdotal reports. Anecdotal reports can be tainted by a host of psychological and sociological factors. They are unreliable.

AR spokesman Arnold Perey, PhD has asserted on the Internet that "...neither "statistics" nor "controlled experiments "are necessary for science." When assessing any type of conversion therapy such methodologies certainly are necessary. At the very least some sort of scientific research should be done. To date, AR has no scientific research to back its claims.

One can only conclude that Siegel's ideas about homosexuality constitute a prejudice on his part. Prejudice (need it be said?) is not science. Siegel's "science" is no more valid than the eugenics of the nineteenth century. But the veneer of science, the illusion that scientific reason has been applied (which is the essence of sacred science) is used by AR disciples to lay claim to legitimacy.

In a *Wikipedia* discussion with AR promoter Arnold Perey, "Marinero" poses this challenge:

If you are truly interested in providing evidence, then let it be quantifiable, scientific evidence. Let your body provide the evidence. Scientists can measure all sorts of bodily reactions to certain stimuli. For instance, they can measure dilation of the pupil when something pleasurable is gazed upon. They can also measure such things as blood flow to the genitals, a faster heartbeat, and changes in breathing in response to sexual stimuli. I propose that the ARists who claim to have changed from homosexuality submit to an experiment in which they are shown sexually explicit images of men and women (separately) while having their bodily reactions monitored. If they are truly confident of their change, and if they truly want to provide "evidence" of this change, they should be happy to participate. Of course, I'm sure they'll have all sorts of reasons for not participating. Either that or they simply won't respond to my challenge.

Asked again for this book if they would take-up the challenge, the AR Foundation failed to respond. In an article about Aesthetic Realism, Charles G. Kast of Gaysweek writes:

The efforts of Kinsey to find people [who had genuinely altered their sexual proclivities]...did manage to turn up a few instances [of people claiming to have gone straight]...But on close examination all examples quickly failed to qualify. In most, it was a matter of sheer suppression: "I used to be a lesbian but now I turn away when temptation knocks."..."I don't even think of men, except when I masturbate." Perhaps... [AR's]..."former homosexuals" would take up the offer of Wardell Pomeroy, who following Kinsey's death, put out a standing offer to administer the Kinsey Research Battery to any person and thus possibly "validate a changed homosexuality."

The Aesthetic Realism Foundation was asked during the writing of this book if any of them had submitted to the Kinsey Research Battery. The ARists did not reply to the inquiry. So: Is AR scientific? Definitely not!

AR and Eugenics

The Free Dictionary defines *eugenics* as: "...the study of methods of improving genetic qualities by selective breeding (especially as applied to human mating). So, does AR practice eugenics? Yes and no. "Changed" followers are pressured to begin relationships with followers of the opposite sex. Periodically, consultants have proposed specific followers that a "changed" disciple can couple with.

In the strictest sense, there's no effort to alter future populations, though children are certainly instructed in the norms of the cult and have been brought to public demonstrations and encouraged to write letters on behalf of AR. AR doesn't breed for an improved population. But any sort of selective coupling smacks of eugenics. Certainly, there's an ethical line that AR crosses.

Loaded Language

Aesthetic Realism has *loaded language* (group buzz-words) aplenty. Cultic language provides members the opportunity to feel insightful, special and superior to others. Sometimes the specialized language consists of common words used in uncommon ways. Here are some typical AR buzz-words:

Contempt: The psychological desire to subjugate the world outside one's own mind. AR posits contempt as the root cause of all forms of insanity and mental health disorders, male homosexuality, lesbianism, eating disorders, epilepsy, cancer, thyroid disease, allergies, stuttering, reading disabilities, gum disease, bad marriages, racism, domestic violence, hemorrhoids, and Republican Party politics.

Adoring contempt: If a queer man was well loved by his mother, Siegel assumed that the man (in childhood) returned the love on the surface but held his mother in contempt internally.

Narrow self: The part of the unconscious mind that wants to have contempt for external reality.

Two selves: AR's pseudo-psychological theory that we human beings have unconscious minds that are divided into two impulses: the desire to embrace or "like" external realities and the desire to depreciate ("have contempt for") external realities.

Get a victory: You get a victory when you have contempt for others. AR presumes, for example, that every youngster who grew up queer "got a victory" over his mother.

Don't use this: When one follower thinks a person's respect for AR might diminish due to some challenging situation, they're told "Don't use this." It's shorthand for "Don't use this to have contempt for Aesthetic Realism and Eli Siegel."

Bilge: Verbal or written statements by anyone who criticizes Aesthetic Realism.

Mr. or Miss: Early in the history of Aesthetic Realism Siegel socialized with his students. Then, he decided they hadn't shown him sufficient respect. He distanced himself socially and insisted that his followers start calling him "Mr. Siegel" instead of "Eli." Followers are also called "Mr." or "Miss" and they rarely address each other by their given names in public.

H or the H persuasion: AR's terms for male homosexuality. They rarely say "gay" or "queer."

L or the L preference: AR's terms for female homosexuality.

Pseudo-lesbian: Any woman who lacked a sexual attraction to other women but who Siegel, in his lifetime, considered to have an excess of antipathy towards men.

Changed: Aesthetic Realists don't like saying that queer people can be "cured." They prefer "changed"—a term that can be applied to other situations as well, such as the purported changes from alcoholism, epilepsy, bulimia, etc.

Poet, critic and philosopher: The honorific often used (with some variations) to describe Eli Siegel.

Philosophy or thought: The terms used to describe Siegel's teachings.

Student, associate, consultant-in-training: A follower. Faithful followers are said to "study" Aesthetic Realism.

Consultant: A senior follower and teacher.

Class chairman: The uber-consultant. Siegel's replacement after his death.

Completely fair: The desire or demand to praise Eli Siegel without any reservations.

The Profit System: Capitalism, which Siegel abhorred. In the 70s, he declared that Capitalism was now grinding to a halt. It hasn't.

Persons: Siegel often used this word instead of "people." His use of words was often stilted and odd.

A making one: As in "beauty is a making one of opposites"—another example of Siegel's bizarre (some would claim "poetic") linguistic affectations. (See the entry for "Persons" above.)

Questions: Actually, questions with predetermined answers that Siegel and other AR leaders often ask in order to impose a point of view on followers. Related: Followers are sometimes "questioned" in meetings, consultations or AR lessons. This means they are criticized and humiliated by and in front of their peers.

Criticism: AR equates this word with the word "love." Anyone who gets upset by being criticized is told that they don't understand that this treatment is really "love."

Gratitude: Unqualified approbation for Eli Siegel, his teachings and for the perceived impact of AR's leaders in one's life.

Regret: Remorse for any perceived moment when a follower's gratitude to Siegel and the cult wavered. Following Siegel's suicide, there was a period of time when disciples couldn't speak-up in a meeting if they didn't begin by offering a statement of regret.

Kind: A description of Siegel or any AR follower who has criticized you; especially if they've criticized you rather brutally.

See/saw/seen: An affirmation that one has come to agree with AR's teachings. As in: "I have seen the truth of Aesthetic Realism."

Represent: The belief held by AR followers that their opinions of the cult and its teachings serve as a stand-in for the future approbation of the entire world; as in: "We represent America which is longing to meet Aesthetic Realism."

The oneness of opposites: The notion that something is beautiful only if it can be shown to resolve opposing abstract qualities. Homosexuality is attacked for failing to combine the opposites of sameness and difference. Siegel asserted that being queer is functionally the same as being a bad work of art. He positioned himself (within his small circle) as the one true judge of world art and literature.

Music: The sound of "true" poetry in Siegel's view. His followers often marveled at his self-proclaimed ability to hear the difference between good poetry and bad when they themselves could not.

Friend: A person who supports AR's ideas without opposition.

Enemy: Former members, members of the media and anyone else who criticizes AR.

Good: A person who praises Eli Siegel and his teachings is said to be "good" about Aesthetic Realism.

Steady: A person who is a longtime and consistent supporter of AR is said to be "steady."

Left: When followers divorce themselves from AR they are said to have "left" Aesthetic Realism.

Met: A follower's first encounter with the cult, as in: "I was twenty-five when I met Aesthetic Realism."

Bad effect: The reason why you should avoid anyone who is not a steadfast supporter of AR. They will cause you to have doubts about the efficacy of the cult's teachings. They will have "a bad effect" on you.

Terror of respect: Siegel's explanation for why people didn't like him. The world (especially the media) rejected him, he claimed, because people feared and hated having to respect his unbounded genius. The "terror of respect" is also the concept Siegel used when alleging that a surgeon had harmed him during surgery. The surgeon, Siegel claimed, hated having to respect him and as a result of this catastrophic, psychological state of affairs the doctor botched the surgery.

Press Boycott of Aesthetic Realism: Siegel's explanation for why he wasn't world famous. He never admitted the fact that folks in the media might simply have considered his opinions to be unworthy of publication since his ideas were never backed by scientific research. Or to put it more rudely: Siegel couldn't face the fact that outsiders perceived him as a kook.

Truth or true: Aesthetic Realists' assertion that their group runs the inside track of enlightened knowledge.

A personal emotion: What female followers experienced when they had sex with Eli Siegel. (More about this later.)

Pills intended for sleep: Siegel's chosen method of suicide. (More about this later.)

Doctrine Over Person

Simply: The group and its teachings come first. Your personal needs come second. Or alternately: If you're a devoted follower then the group's needs are your needs and nothing will come ahead of that. Ex-followers have complained that AR co-opted their lives. They were pressured to avoid non-supporters (including relatives who weren't sufficiently effusive), to attend AR's frequent (often paid) events and to live near the AR Foundation, usually with other followers.

An example: One former follower (let's call him Jonah) who was born into the cult complained that he was discouraged from attending college. He was already studying the greatest knowledge in the world, he was told. Why then did he need to go to college?

One AR leader attempted to discredit Jonah's complaint with this online rebuttal: "I knew [Jonah]...from the time he was about four years old...From an early age, he did not respect learning sufficiently... [Jonah] pointed to a row of...children's books and said Mr. Siegel had given these to him..."I never read them," Jonah said."

Dredging up Jonah's perceived early childhood flaws is supposed to prove that Jonah is an unreliable witness. The AR leader's condemnation of Jonah is petty. This little "teaching story" also inadvertently reveals something else: Siegel was ineffective at getting young Jonah interested in reading. So much for AR's claim that it can "end the crisis in education."

Dispensing of Existence

Basically: We're enlightened; you're not. John Stacey describes the phenomenon this way: "Only group members are really "walking in the light," know the "truth," or are in "the Kingdom of God"—while others are somehow negative and excluded."

AR members pity those who will not join or who have escaped the group. It is not uncommon to hear followers say of an ex-member: "He can't possibly have a true emotion, now." Faithful followers have "seen the truth of" Aesthetic Realism. They will be "teaching the world" someday. An AR print ad once proclaimed: *The Aesthetic Realism of Eli Siegel is True.*

Those who don't exemplify the "truth" of Aesthetic Realism are cast out. This includes queer people who fall off the wagon. But there are others who are ostracized as well. Athena Kouletsis, an AR teacher committed the ultimate sin: She got cancer. Eli Siegel claimed he understood the cause of cancer (contempt for the world expressed as a desire to separate oneself from the world). He and his followers believed that through AR cancer could be cured. Tragically for Athena, this turned out not to be true. As her body wasted away, AR leaders forbade her from attending functions at the AR Foundation. They didn't want evidence of Athena's disrespect (her fatal illness) to be witnessed by other followers.

Athena Kouletsis was one of several cancer patients who were warned away from the AR Foundation. Followers with other illnesses were berated for having doctor-recommended operations rather than "changing their attitudes to the world" through Aesthetic Realism. A former AR consultant reports that one cancer patient was encouraged by AR leaders to commit suicide so that the evidence of this insider's disrespect for Eli Siegel would vanish quickly from view.

When followers get ill many AR leaders can be relied upon to dispense with compassion. AR disciples think of themselves as possessing an abiding respect for the world and its people. Their actions towards sick members belie this conviction.

Two

Siegel, Sex and Hypocrisy

These are the primary assertions Siegel put forth about homosexuality as published in *The Aesthetic Realism of Eli Siegel and the Change from Homosexuality*:

- All homosexuality arises from contempt of the world.

- This changes to contempt for women.

Siegel wrote of female homosexuality in AR's in-house newsletter *The Right of Aesthetic Realism to Be Known* (Number 543):

- No girl becomes a lesbian if she has respect for the world as she has come to know it. This has been ascertained through consultations...

- A lesbian is a mingling of contempt for the male sex...and a desire to have the advantages of the male sex...

In *The Right of Aesthetic Realism to Be Known* (Number 503)
there is this gem: "Eli Siegel related a homosexual son and his
mother to Bonnie and Clyde—two people who, because they care
for each other, have to shoot up the rest of the world."

Siegel's teachings about homosexuality fit neatly into the FBI's
definition of sexual-orientation bias: "A preformed negative
opinion or attitude toward a group of persons based on their
sexual attraction toward, and responsiveness to, members of their
own sex or members of the opposite sex, e.g., gays, lesbians,
heterosexuals."

Queer followers of AR are told, in so-called Aesthetic Realism
lessons with Eli Siegel and in consultations that they are riddled
with contempt for the world. Every life-choice, every example of
personal history is viewed as proof of this. You're not really "H"
(homosexual) followers are told. You're really straight but covered
over with near-impenetrable layers of contempt. It is recorded in
The H Persuasion that Siegel told one of his earliest disciples:
"[Homosexuality] is a superstructure you built on to yourself...you
think it is you. I don't think it is." By exposing oneself to
criticism, AR claims, a queer person can dig through the
contemptuous psychological layers to find his or her true,
heterosexual self.

What goes on in AR consultations? It's a little like therapy, a little
like confession. Consultations consist of a series of questions that
presuppose contempt for the world. Leaders never exhibit a real
desire to know and understand the "consultee." One is expected to

agree with the implications of each question, or to ask the kind of clarifying questions that demonstrate a willingness to enter into a deeper level of agreement. [Ed.: You'll see this in Appendix Three which contains the complete transcript of an AR consultation.]

Queer men are always presumed inferior to straight or "changed" men—no matter how bad those other men may be. And queer men are doomed if they don't know and accept AR's teachings. One "changed" follower, Russ, was told that "all" queer men would die of AIDS. Russ also writes: "...the beginning of the end for me was when I got into a crazy argument with [the consultants] about a straight man raping a woman. Their notion was...yes, rape is bad. But at least the rapist is not "H" and therefore knows the world better than I ever could."

AR consultants and Siegel before them have never admitted failure in the field of homosexuality. In this and other fields, failure is blamed on the individual. Estelle Feingold, the wife of a "changed" man reports that her husband Irwin finally admitted to her that he'd been mistaken about changing from homosexuality. Irwin later admitted this to Siegel himself. Siegel asked, "Have you had an emotion for Mrs. Feingold?" "Yes," Irwin answered. "Then you've changed."

Siegel's homophobia ran so deep that he simply couldn't conceive of the fact that a queer man can care for a woman without being sexually attracted to her. And of course to admit that Irwin Feingold was telling the truth would be to admit failure. This never happens in AR. The men are blamed, and even ejected from the group, if they won't go on the record (and stay there) as having changed from homosexuality.

Appendix Four presents a complete, full-length inquisition in which a lapsed "changed" man is raked over the coals and asked to leave both the group and New York City in order to hide AR's failure. Two briefer statements are below. The first is from a man who was ousted because AR had failed to change his homosexuality:

I was a student for about two and a half years from summer 1987 until the end of 1989. The experience was strange to say the least, and the word cult often crossed my mind while I was "studying." I began to study because I was gay and it was not cool to be gay in a rural area not to mention my parents are devout Catholic...I learned early on that if I didn't express gratitude for AR and ES often I would be in trouble. Looking back I can't believe I lasted there as long as I did. It happened to be my fourth one, and most of the hour was spent on how I wasn't grateful enough for AR and [AR founder] Eli Siegel. When I protested that I hadn't changed yet I was told that I had seen enough already of the great beauty of AR. During the consultation I was asked very leading questions like how did I think about myself after being attracted to another man. Did I think more or less of myself? Did I think more or less of the other person? (Now how would any twenty-two-year-old Catholic closet case answer these questions?) At no time was I given any numbers as to how many people had changed. I was just told "many people had changed." I was also never told how long I should expect to study before I would change, nor for that matter that people who had changed had recanted. I was afraid to ask these questions because of the element of fear that if I wasn't respectful enough they would drop me.

They dropped me anyway. My consultants eventually told me I couldn't study any more. They said I wasn't trying hard enough and I was thwarting their efforts. They were very rude when they did this and I was devastated...I can understand they were disappointed that I hadn't changed after two and half years of study, but since they always claimed to have good will for me I would think they would have said something nicer like, "We feel we have done all we can for you for now and encourage you to continue to study on your own."... That was a long time ago and I now feel I am a reasonably well adjusted gay man and am out to just about everyone I know.

The next statement demonstrates AR's obsession with "gratitude"—and money:

The one thing that really seems a racket to me is how they tell you that you are not ready to express gratitude when you say you haven't changed from homosexuality and maybe if you would donate some money it would help. I cannot believe that they are denying that they led us to believe they could change people from H as they called it. I was there in the early 80's and gay people outnumbered the straight people and changing from homosexuality was one of the main topics.

What About Sex?

There isn't much. It's difficult at best for the men who "changed."
Sure, it happens to some degree. And in some cases children are
produced. But here's what former followers have said:

Coleen [About her husband Benjamin]: "It was all he could do to
get it up, stick it in and get it over with."

Beverly [About her husband Gregg]: "He admitted to me he'd
made a mistake about changing from H. The only way I could
even get him out of his room was to start baking cookies. Then,
he'd come out and bake with me."

Alex [Shortly after his marriage to Caitlin]: "I still don't associate
the same feeling of being hot with women that I did with men."

Roberta [Criticizing her husband Lee at an AR group meeting for
their lack of a sex life]: "I think a wife has a right to expect a
reasonable amount of sex from her husband."

Don [About a night he spent with Sarah]: "We didn't actually have
sex. We talked a lot about whether we should; then before we
knew it it was dawn."

Violet [Who dated consultant-in-training Myron for six months and consultant Zach for another six]: "I never had sex with either of them. After months Zach and I never got past kissing."

Many, many AR followers resumed having queer sex after disassociating from AR. Some resumed their lives before they left. Murray, a former insider, tells of presenting a paper about his "change" at the Aesthetic Realism Foundation. Two nights later, Murray and Burt (a consultant who was teaching other men to "change" from homosexuality) had sex. Appendix Four demonstrates what can happen to an AR follower if he resumes having queer sex. "Luke Randall" was drummed out of AR, but not before undergoing an excruciating and cruel inquisition.

The screaming and vitriol in this session are typical of many AR meetings in the 70s and 80s, even when someone wasn't being expelled. Siegel wasn't above doing it himself. Even with children. Even with his wife. His neighbors were perturbed by his periodic verbal assaults on Martha Baird Siegel. They complained to the landlady. [Ed.: The landlady was vilified by Siegel's followers after his death. There were street demonstrations in front of her office because she refused to sell the building to Siegel's followers so they could turn it into a shrine.]

Luke Randall wasn't the only follower to be expelled from the group. There were other queer men, an alcoholic who fell off the wagon, and a female leader who wanted to go public about her longtime affair with Eli Siegel.

There is ample evidence that Aesthetic Realism is a failure where the "change" from homosexuality is concerned. Despite this, cult leaders continue to defend their unsupported position. On their website called *Countering the Lies* the group writes:

The Friends of Aesthetic Realism...will not...say that no one really changed from homosexuality through study of Aesthetic Realism, and that Aesthetic Realism was wrong on the subject. Men and women have changed; the change is real, and full.

It is typical of AR that they provide no scientific research to support this assertion. They ignore the ex-followers who now say that they were mistaken in their claims to have changed from homosexuality. There are also queer followers still in the group who confided in others (while those others were still members) that they had difficulties having sex with members of the opposite sex.

It is important to note that the above statement from the *Friends of Aesthetic Realism* is more than just a defense of their junk science. It is an avowal of bigotry. By refusing to say that AR is "wrong on the subject" of homosexuality the cult defends its claim that queerness is an ethical failing, a manifestation of contempt for the world and the opposite sex. This avowal places Aesthetic Realism squarely in the pantheon of hate groups.

AR disciples claim that they support gay rights. Their leader, Eli Siegel, did not, at least when out of public view. Of the Gay

Liberation Movement he said to his followers: "H [homosexuality] has gotten into its smug period." The struggle against discrimination, the struggle for fairness in housing and the workplace and against unwarranted incarceration and assault was reduced to that one word: smug.

One right of all human beings is the freedom from being targets of bigotry. Eli Siegel did not offer this freedom to the LGBT community; his followers don't offer this freedom either. They are the purveyors of contempt; not the queer community.

No Ethics Here

Siegel was the first in line to condemn queer people for their "contemptuous" sexual ethics; yet he was hardly a saint in this field. He had, in his lifetime, a string of affairs with female followers. As he described it, these women were having a "personal emotion" for him. Later in life, when maintaining an erection was no longer possible, women in the group (always the most beautiful) were invited to sit naked on Siegel's lap and play with his genitals.

Toben and Helge (*Sexual Misconduct of Clergypersons with Congregants or Parishioners: Civil and Criminal Liabilities and Responsibilities*) write that "...the existence of a fiduciary relationship between the counselor and the client...calls for the fiduciary (the counselor) to fully subordinate his or her interests to the interests of the client...In such a case, the relationship of trust...reliance, emotional intimacy, and vulnerability, that is recognized as necessarily characterizing a...counseling relationship [must not be] meaningfully in question once the relationship is defined."

Siegel's dalliances constitute an egregious betrayal of trust. One might well argue that he is the last person to speak authoritatively on the subject of sexual ethics

Harm Done

In 1973, at the height of AR's anti-homosexual campaign a world-changing event occurred. The American Psychological Association (APA) declassified homosexuality as a mental disorder. Activists had opened the APA's eyes to the fact that queer people who went for therapy had other morbidities coincidental to their homosexuality and these had brought them into treatment. But there were many happy, well-adjusted homosexuals who the therapists hadn't seen by virtue of the fact that the queer silent majority felt no need for therapy.

Eli Siegel and his followers however continued to insist that LGBT people needed changing. They continued to give lessons and consultations to the more dysfunctional members of the LGBT community. Schidlo, Schroeder and Drescher (*Sexual Conversion Therapy: Ethical, Clinical, and Research Perspectives*) say: "Disturbingly...in their ideological or religious zeal...to create heterosexuals reparative or conversion therapists tend to overlook or dismiss any possible harmful side effects of such treatments."

Siegel and his acolytes ignored symptoms of depression and anxiety in their queer consultees. In fact, they weren't qualified to treat these people in the first place. Aesthetic Realists would claim that AR isn't therapy; it's "education." Regardless of such assertions, consultations and AR lessons have always held a pseudo-therapeutic tinge. The minute you start counseling people on sexual issues, relationship issues, substance abuse issues and the like you're in therapy mode.

When unqualified people take it upon themselves to do therapy they can inflict a lot of damage on others. Darren Lapinsky is one such individual. Darren attended a Bible college in the late 70s. One of his instructors was an Aesthetic Realist who threatened to "out" him if he didn't take consultations and become heterosexual.

Darren, as a teenager, had been thrown out of his Seventh Day Adventist high school for being gay. His family institutionalized him and Darren was pumped-up on Thorazine. When that didn't make him straight his parents tossed him out. So when Darren's instructor threatened to "out" him it brought up serious anxieties and precipitated an emotional crisis.

Under duress, Darren traveled four hours each way, week after week, to take unwanted consultations at AR headquarters. He had nearly seventy consultations. These did not alter his sexual preferences. In fact, Darren's desire for men grew stronger during this period. But the consultations did have consequences. Darren was so depressed by the psychological attacks he endured at the hands of his AR consultants that he began drinking. For years after his AR experience he drank heavily until he finally sought the help of a cult-recovery counselor.

Darren gave his counselor some of his recorded consultations to listen to. She was shocked. "I'm surprised you survived," she told him. "They fucked your mind over. No wonder you're so dysfunctional." As a cult expert, Darren's counselor clearly recognized the psychological destructiveness of AR's pseudo-therapy sessions.

"It felt like I was being interrogated," Darren said of his consultations. "The light was so low I could barely see their faces. They frequently made fun of my looks. I had long, blond hair back then, and looked like a California surfer. They told me I was contemptuous of the world because of my looks. Later, when I asked why I wasn't changing they told me it was because I was not grateful enough to Eli Siegel. I didn't even know the man, but they said I wasn't changing because I didn't recognize how wonderful and powerful Eli Siegel was."

Even today, nearly four decades after he escaped the cult, Darren Lapinsky is haunted by the memories of his AR experience.

There's no evidence that Siegel and his consultants ever gave a moment's thought to whether or not they were qualified to do their pseudo-therapeutic work. Certainly, they never exposed their methods to the scrutiny of professionals by publishing in peer-reviewed journals or by presenting their seminar papers at professional psychology conferences. When challenged on the subject of homosexuality, they ultimately decided to stop discussing the topic in public.

In his lifetime, Siegel never publicly defended his pseudo-psychological queer-bashing. He preferred to hide behind his followers' metaphorical skirts whenever it came time for a public seminar or television appearance. Siegel chose to teach only in his own home and only nestled safely in the bosom of his flock. Even then he taught only the inner circle. The insiders then went out and taught others.

The Aesthetic Realists continued their homophobic work for years even though the APA had made it clear that homosexuality was perfectly normal. It's harder, these days, to ply one's homophobic trade in a progressive neighborhood like SoHo, New York, so AR's disciples have no choice but to keep their homophobia under wraps.

Certainly, their self-imposed silence would indicate that they're running scared. They are, after all, living in one of the world's largest LGBT communities.

In recent years, other health organizations have followed the APA in their condemnation of conversion therapy; yet Siegel's disciples have neither retracted nor modified their stance on homosexuality. They were offered the opportunity to do so as this book was being written.

Additionally, since it is possible that Aesthetic Realists still engage in verbal queer bashing behind closed doors, anyone who comes among them can be tainted. This doesn't only mean new members. Many Aesthetic Realists teach in public schools. Their negativity can spill-out into their classrooms.

Disciples who teach can potentially bash their LGBT students either verbally or through a myriad of "under-the-radar" attacks—anything from indifference to derisive body language to excessive criticism. The attacks don't have to be explicitly about queerness to be about queerness. All of these teacher behaviors would endanger the well-and-good of queer students.

Here are some position statements from major health organizations regarding conversion therapies:

The American Medical Association (AMA):

"[The AMA]...opposes the use of "reparative" or "conversion" therapy that is based upon the assumption that homosexuality per se is a mental disorder or based on the a priori assumption that the patient should change his/her homosexual orientation."

The Pan-American Health Organization (PAHO):

"Services that purport to "cure" people with non-heterosexual orientation lack medical justification and represent a serious threat to the health and well-being of affected people..."

The World Health Organization:

The World Health Organization concurs with PAHO's conclusions and has posted PAHO's position statement on its website. One of the points posted on the site says that "'Conversion' or 'reparative' therapies and the clinics offering them should be denounced and subject to adequate sanctions."

The harm done by cults, homophobic or otherwise is manifold. Cult members build a sense of meaning around their particular groups. Separation can lead to a loss of one's sense of mission. It can also mean that the dissolution of some, if not all of one's friendships. A profound sense of loss, under such circumstances is natural.

Counseling may be required. Survivors (with or without the help of a therapist) must develop a plan to reintegrate into larger society. This may mean reconnecting with former friends and estranged relatives; seeking out new social activities; and finding new activities that can bring one a sense of mission and accomplishment.

Guilt and shame are prevalent among survivors. These may include shame for having participated in a cult, shame for leaving the cult or some combination of the two. Again, recognizing the problem is an important first step. Seeking professional help may be crucial in many cases.

Rick Ross notes that ex-cult members sometimes experience severe panic attacks. He warns that if you are experiencing four or more of the following symptoms, you may be having a panic attack:

- Pounding heart
- Sweating
- Trembling or shaking
- Shortness of breath or a feeling of smothering
- Feeling of choking
- Chest pain or discomfort
- Nausea or abdominal distress

- Feeling dizzy, unsteady, light-headed or faint

- Feelings of de-realization (surroundings don't seem real)

- Depersonalization (feeling detached)

- Fear of losing control or going crazy

- Fear of dying

- Numbness, tingling, and hot and cold flashes

If you are a cult survivor and you think you are suffering from panic attacks, seek-out medical attention immediately.

A common problem among survivors is the fear of retaliation. Sometimes, this can be an over-dramatization but sometimes it can be real. AR is one group that is retaliatory in nature. They have held public demonstrations in front of the homes of reporters and other "enemies." They have named names online. Former members are aware of these retaliatory efforts and they're nervous. This is why many of them insisted on anonymity when contributing to this book and to Michael Bluejay's website.

A Social-Addictive Disorder

Jansa and Perlado (*Annual Conference of the European Federation of Centers for Research and Information on Cults*, 2004) identify cult membership as a social-addictive disorder similar to drug addiction. When you leave a cult you are essentially in a state of withdrawal. Some people can tough it out alone, but many can't. The latter should seek therapeutic help.

If you're an ex-Aesthetic Realist you didn't need help "changing" your homosexuality. Not that that was ever possible. But you may need to fix the residual psychological damage done by the cult. If you can't go it alone, please don't hesitate to find a queer-affirmative therapist.

A note of warning: Therapy is a consumer service. If you find a therapist and he/she isn't helping, then feel no guilt about seeking someone new. Keep in mind that you once ceded your personal power to someone else. Don't fall into that trap with a therapist. Therapists are required by the rules of professional ethics to serve your needs, not to impose theirs. If a therapist isn't meeting your needs, move on.

The important thing to remember is that there is life after a cult. You will find a new, rich, meaningful life if you make the effort to do so; and if you seek help should you find yourself floundering.

For more information about recovery, Appendix Five offers a list of resources.

Three

Siegel's Death

Eli Siegel's greatest victim was Eli Siegel. His wife, Martha Baird Siegel was also his victim. As previously reported Siegel verbally abused his wife and cuckolded her with younger women. In the end, he asked her to die with him.

Siegel committed suicide. In 1978, he needed surgery for a prostate condition. Believing his own hype he convinced himself that no doctor could understand his mind or his body. So he avoided medical treatment for months, choosing to live in agony.

Finally, some of his closest followers prevailed upon him to seek medical attention. He needed an operation. His followers pressured him into having it.

After the operation, Siegel complained that he couldn't "feel" his feet. He'd had problems beforehand but they became acute after the surgery. Neuropathy is a common side effect of some surgical procedures. It may be caused by "...mechanical factors, such as compression, stretch, contusion or transection..." or in some cases by inflammation (*Brain: A Journal of Neurology*, August 3rd,

2010). Siegel may have suffered from neuropathy which was further exacerbated by the surgery.

This collateral effect of surgery is unfortunate, but in no way does it constitute malpractice. Siegel, however, accused the surgeon of "ruining his life." A charge was filed, an investigation opened, and the hospital found no evidence of wrongdoing.

This didn't stop Siegel from making accusations. Nor did it stop him from laying a massive guilt trip on his disciples. He blamed them for forcing the surgery on him. Siegel told his inner circle that he wanted to die.

A variety of statements made by Siegel after the surgery (e.g. "What once had color is covered over with gray.") indicate that he may have been suffering from clinical depression. A document written by his followers (*On the Dying of Eli Siegel*) adds fuel to this theory. The document says that after Siegel's operation "...he was not able to sleep," and that Siegel "...found that he could not read..." Sleep problems and difficulty with concentration are typical of clinically depressed people. And suicidal thoughts are clear indicators of a mental health crisis. Sadly, when you fancy yourself the chief interpreter of all psychological maladies, it's hard to admit that you're having problems and that you need the help of a legitimate professional.

The surgeon, Siegel claimed had been overcome by the "terror of respect" and as a result Dr. X made a mistake during the surgery.

Siegel's followers then, and to this day, beat their breasts over leading him to slaughter, as they perceive it.

"Mr. Siegel did not want the operation," his followers write (*On the Dying of Eli Siegel*). "...had we not wanted to feel we knew better than Mr. Siegel, had we not wanted somewhere to be superior to him, we would have had a different kind of thought about this operation." What was their alternative? Let him die of prostate cancer?

Siegel's inner circle also began a letter-writing campaign demanding that the poor surgeon "come clean" about harming "the greatest man in human history," a man who couldn't possibly be understood by doctors because he had "a different relation of mind and body" from anyone else in history. (This from the people who also insist they don't view Siegel as a god.)

In a poem called *Let Us Pray for True Knowledge*, Siegel wrote: "Sometimes the way body and mind explain each other is different from what has been/I see myself as a trembling victim of insufficient knowledge accompanied by more than sufficient complacency."

Siegel bought-into his own myth, convincing himself that his mind and body were different from those of other human beings. He was self-delusional and in the end, self-destructive.

69

Pills Intended for Sleep

Siegel's wife reported that her husband had asked her (the woman he'd abused and betrayed) to join him in death. Much to the ire of some of Siegel's loyal followers she turned him down. Some of Siegel's inner-circle felt that Miss Baird (as she was known) had disrespected her great husband by remaining alive.

Over time, pressure was brought to bear and Baird, who suffered from severe health problems, was worn down. She too killed herself but not before she annoyed some of the inner-circle by demanding a last supper—a hamburger, well-done. "A hamburger? Well-done? Why doesn't she just get it over with?" one follower is reported to have said.

Siegel's suicide was not discussed away from the inner-circle. The official word was that he "died of a broken heart" because the world never came knocking at his door. It never has. It probably never will.

It's not surprising that Siegel's followers avoid discussion of his suicide other than to say he "died with dignity." And even this confession was evaded for years until Michael Bluejay's website forced the issue into the open. What the Aesthetic Realists don't discuss is the fact that many of them took a role in Siegel's death. A former AR consultant reports that insiders helped Siegel to die by going to their doctors and complaining of sleep trouble. Each participant then delivered a bottle of "pills intended for sleep" (in

Martha Baird's words) so that Baird could choose a bottle at random and give it to her husband.

Nobody knew which bottle actually killed Siegel. Followers reasoned that if they didn't know whose pills were used, then none of them had to feel guilty. To outsiders this would seem to be a twisted rationalization. But to Siegel's followers it made perfect sense. After Siegel's death, all of the bottles were removed from the home of the couple with whom the cult leader had been staying in his final days.

One can only breathe a sigh of relief that Martha Baird was the only follower asked to join Siegel in death. Considering the breast-beating going on at the time this could easily have become another Jonestown.

Eli Siegel's Legacy

Eli Siegel's legacy is one of junk science, unchecked vanity and harm to the LGBT community. His life is a cautionary tale of the effects of homophobia on victims and perpetrators. The world has gone on. Homophobia is still rabid and rampant, but the Gay Rights Movement has advanced, too. Homosexuality is not a dark, shameful secret for many. It is simply part of who we are. We have friends, we have family, and we have love and acceptance. We have lives.

Many others will document the evils of homophobia and the joys of queer lives when they are fully actualized. Other writers will tell their tales. The work of queer scholars, writers, artists and politicians will continue. To borrow a phrase from Eli Siegel's tombstone, the good work of strong, articulate queer people and their allies will be "continued by the world."

Appendix One
I'm from Driftwood

An earlier version of his article was first published on the website called *I'm from Driftwood* (www.imfromdriftwood.com) on August 5th, 2011.

I am a survivor of Aesthetic Realism, one of the world's first "ex-gay" cults. I came of age in the '70s, the victim of lots of derision. I was constantly reminded by my family and schoolmates that I wasn't good at sports, that I had a funny, high voice, that I acted "like a girl."

My mother feared that I would be queer, so from an early age I was screamed at and punished whenever I attempted to play with girls. This was her way of trying to keep me straight. I even remember being sent to my room and made to sit for hours in silence because I'd talked to a girl who lived in our Bronx apartment house.

To me being queer meant being a victim. I wanted to fit in. So when I started taking acting classes in Greenwich Village, and my teacher announced that her husband was the "first man to change from homosexuality" through Aesthetic Realism, I jumped at the chance to join up. I convinced my parents to pay for AR encounter groups, which the cult calls "consultations." AR promised to relieve my self-loathing. I bought-in.

I started taking Aesthetic Realism consultations. Here's how they worked. You sat in a booth facing three self-hating homosexuals. They would then teach you the principles of AR: You were homosexual because you had contempt for your mother. This extended to all other women. By having contempt for women, you were by extension having contempt for the whole world. Homosexuality, in other words, was the result of an erroneous world-view and an ethical failing.

It was pure crap, but to a desperate and depressed late-adolescent it sounded plausible. I was told that if I allowed them to "criticize" my contempt for the world and women I would, in time, become heterosexual. I heard all sorts of trash talk about my relationship with my mother, my abusive father (whom they praised for standing up to my "contempt for women"); and when my brother, a doctor, raised questions about the efficacy of AR, the three self-haters demanded that I break off my relationship with him.

Anyone who asked serious questions or posed serious challenges was "an enemy" to AR and should be avoided, including members of your immediate family. You had to prove your loyalty by constant, effusive statements of praise to Eli Siegel, the cult's founder. You were "encouraged" to write letters praising Siegel, which provided him, of course, with reams of testimonials.

After a year of consultations, I confessed that I still felt queer. I was having sexual thoughts about another male group member. One of the consultants giggled nervously and said, "You'd be surprised at who still has those thoughts." I was then served the standard AR excuse: I was having queer fantasies because I hated my "gratitude" to Eli Siegel and therefore wanted to make him look bad.

I learned that many of the men who'd gone "straight" eventually quit the cult and returned to a queer lifestyle. One man who married and later had a child confided in me that sex with his wife was never as "hot" as it was with men. I heard from some of the "changed" men's wives and girlfriends that their sex lives were pathetic. One woman confided that her husband hated having sex but loved making cookies with her.

After years of hiding the fact that I was still queer, thinking it was a failing on my part, I gathered the courage to quit AR. It wasn't easy. Escaping a cult never is. The indoctrination process creates a lot of internal pressure. One AR leader told me, "You can leave; but one has to like oneself."

Members warned me that if I quit the cult I might lose my mind, or my mother might die of cancer. (The logic of that one was never explained.) After escaping, I sought treatment. With the support of a good therapist, I was de-programmed from AR, came out of the closet and claimed my manhood. I have led a productive life as a teacher, author and openly queer adoptive parent and grandfather. Do I like myself, now? You bet!

Appendix Two

A Public Proclamation

The names have been redacted, but following is the *New York Times* advertisement in which a group of Siegel's followers, most of whom later reclaimed their queerness, proclaimed that they had become heterosexual through Aesthetic Realism. The author included his name in this ad. That claim is herein retracted.

This ad appeared in the *New York Times*, May 3, 1979; *Washington Post*, May 8, 1979; *Los Angeles Times*, May 22, 1979. (First printed in *New York Times* 3/30/78; 4/23/78)

The New York Times Magazine

June 3, 1979

Advertisement   Advertisement

Appendix Three

An Aesthetic Realism Consultation

This is the transcript of a tape-recorded AR telephone consultation. The names of the individuals involved have been changed. The consultation clearly demonstrates AR's contempt for homosexuals as well as the consultants' obsession over eliciting effusive gratitude to Siegel.

DT: Aesthetic Realism consultation of Ben Cangelosi, August 31st, 1987, with Aesthetic Realism consultants Dennis Winterbourne, Nate Lefkowitz and Dwayne Timmons.

NL: Hello, Mr. Cangelosi.

BC: Hello.

NL: This is Nate Lefkowitz.

BC: Hello.

DW: This is Dennis Winterbourne.

DT: And this is Mr. Timmons. Hello, Mr. Cangelosi.

BC: Hello.

DT: The first thing we'd like to tell you about is that there's been a great review, a tremendous fine, honest review of the book The Aesthetic Realism of Eli Siegel and the Change from Homosexuality printed in the Long Island paper called *The Beacon*. It's Long Island's largest weekly circulation newspaper. And it was published in this week's issue. And the review was written by a man who was changed from homosexuality through the study of Aesthetic Realism. The man is Timothy Lynch. So we're very, very glad the paper has published this review informing people throughout the area of the book, its value, describing its contents, and also, uh, Mr. Lynch in the review talks about his own life and the effect of Aesthetic Realism and the study of Aesthetic Realism has had on him. So we're very glad for this and the fact that people throughout the Long Island area are seeing this review. Are you familiar with New York and Long Island? [Ed.: Note that Timothy Lynch is an AR follower and not an unbiased reviewer.]

BC: No, I'm not at all.

DT: I see. Well, uh, part of New York, is, um, well, uh, New York City is on the very edge, end of Long Island, it's technically part of Long Island, and the rest of the, outside of the city is all the suburbs of Nassau County and Suffolk County. Um, and again this is the largest weekly circulation paper on Long Island. So, it's a very fine thing and I hope you'll be hearing more about it. One thing that Mr. Lynch says in the review is that this book should be in every single school library in the country and I agree with him, and he also gives his opinion of Mr. Siegel as being unparalleled in history with his desire to know, his scholarship, and his understanding of the self and mind of man. So it's a great review. We're very, very glad for it.

BC: Congratulations.

NL: Well, it's congratulations, yes, but this is something tremendously important and beautiful that happens that we don't know how many thousands of people including homosexual men will read this and have a chance to know the knowledge you're learning and to change their lives so, so much. So it's very, very important.

DW: And it's important for your life too, Mr. Cangelosi, because it is a means of your "self" being backed up, your high opinion of Mr. Siegel and Aesthetic Realism being encouraged as it should be, and the point is that this article should have... well, it should have been sooner. It should be in other newspapers, and it will. And meanwhile, this is an important development. So we wanted to ask as this consultation begins, what stood out for you in your last consultation?

BC: Well I think the thing that stood out for me most was when you told me the thing that any homosexual feelings I had toward another man would be contempt, or ill will toward him.

DW: Yes.

BC: I don't think I fully understand it yet, but I think that's the thing that most, you know, hit me most.

DT: In what way did it affect you, when you say that's what stood out the most, what do you mean?

BC: Well, I guess it's the thing that, you know, you told me that I would be most surprised at, because I didn't see it as ill will or contempt before.

NL: So why do you think, Mr. Cangelosi, you always felt so badly about the homosexual feelings you had, had the shame, and you want so much to change them? Not to have them anymore? If you just had them in your mind certainly society didn't know about them. I don't think you told anybody. And yet it made you feel very not good. Dirty. I remember having these feelings myself, for years. So why do you think that something in yourself was so against that, so ashamed of it?

BC: Because, I felt that, um, I knew it was wrong inside.

DW: But what do you think that comes from, the feeling that it's wrong inside?

BC: Well, the part of me, the conscience, that wants to do what's right and what's just.

DW: So do you think that what's right and what's just has to do with respect and contempt?

BC: Yes.

DW: And do you think that when a person feels he hasn't done something right, it comes from... and this is made conscious through the study of Aesthetic Realism. But that it's because a person has been unjust to another person or the world?

BC: Right.

DW: And that is contempt.

DT: So do you think that is true? As you thought about it you said that's what affected you, what we said, but do you think that's true about your life? Do you think that as you've thought about men in the past, do you think your purpose was to respect them and the world more, or to have contempt for them, as you thought about them that way?

BC: It was... It was for contempt.

DT: Okay. So how do you see that? So how do you see that being true about your life?

BC: Because, um, because I wasn't trying to respect them or the world more.

DT: And in what way, as you thought about this, what did you think about it? How were you not trying to respect them more?

BC: [Silence]

DT: Do you think that you wanted to know, uh, a man as you thought about him?

BC: No.

DT: So do you think you were interested in using him for your, uh, pleasure of feeling for those moments that you were the most important, powerful thing in the world? As he crumbled for you, as you conquered him in your mind?

BC: [Silence]

DT: Do you think you were not interested in knowing him, but interested in using him to make yourself superior?

BC: Well I was interested in, ah, you know, using him for my own purposes. But I really have a hard time with, you know, "trying to make myself superior."

DT: So what was your purpose? What were the purposes that you're referring to?

BC: Well, for pleasure, for sexual pleasure.

DT: Right. Now, what was the nature of the pleasure? Do you think that the nature of the pleasure... do you think that as you had pleasure thinking about a man, did you like yourself for the pleasure you had?

BC: No.

DT: All right. It's crucial for a person to get all the pleasure he can in this world, and at the same time respect himself for it. That's what Aesthetic Realism says. Our purpose is to have all the pleasure the world can give us, all the pleasure we can get from the world, and simultaneously think more of ourselves and the world as a result. So do you think your purposes, as you thought about a man that way, do you think you were interested in who he was?

BC: No.

DT: So then do you think you were, as you thought about a man, and you conquered him in your mind, had your way with him, do you think you felt then more important? [Ed.: Note that even though Ben Cangelosi expressed uncertainty about the AR explanation of homosexuality, the consultants have ignored him and continue to impose the AR viewpoint on him.]

BC: [Silence]

DT: For those minutes?

BC: I...I don't know if I did or not.

DT: Well, did you think you were some weak, pathetic person, or do you think for those moments you had some strong, aloof man crumble for you, yield to you? Do you think you were something like the ruler of the world for those moments?

BC: Yeah, but I guess I don't see him crumbling, either.

DW: Well he was doing what you wanted him to do, right? He had no say in the matter?

BC: Well...it wasn't like I forced him.

DT: No. As you think about having your way with a man...

BC: Yeah?

DT: Do you think the height of the pleasure is feeling that for those moments that you're affecting him, he's almost mindless about you? He's in such a state of excitement and frenzy that he's almost mindless about you?

BC: I have a hard time seeing that, or thinking that I feel that way.

DT: Well, as you think about a man and a man yields to you, unless you do to him whatever you want, is he just cool, or is he all worked up? In your mind as you think about him?

BC: He's probably worked up.

DT: Probably?

BC: Well, yeah.

DT: Let's... come on, what are we talking about? So he's worked up.

BC: Right.

DT: And what is he worked up over, the cornfields or you?

BC: Me.

DT: You. So do you think for those moments you're having, you're making somebody all worked up, all in a fluster, not sensible, and certainly not cool and calm? Do you think that's true?

BC: Yeah.

DT: So do you think for those moments you feel more powerful, because of the effect you're having on a person?

BC: [Pause] Okay.

DT: Do you get the mailman to respond that way? Or do you get someone in the local supermarket to respond that way when you buy the groceries? Or are they more sensible about you then?

BC: Sensible.

DT: That's right. So do you think as you're thinking about somebody in a homosexual way, and you're, and the person's getting worked up, do you think for those moments you're getting somebody who seems to be strong, otherwise cool, otherwise sensible, for those moments he's in a whirlwind over you?

BC: [Long pause] Okay, I never really thought about it.

DT: Well, is that... is that what happens as you think about a man?

NL: And in the last consultation you mentioned a man named Troy, is that right?

BC: Right.

NL: Now, and he's been used in your mind, is that right?

BC: Right.

NL: He was an instance you gave. At the moment after there has been getting what you wanted, as you call it, pleasure, how did Troy look after?

BC: I never really think about it.

NL: But, do you think that right after the sexual expression, however it was come to, with or without him, do you think he looked stronger to you or weaker?

BC: [Silence]

NL: Do you think that... I don't know just what went on in your mind, and uh things are different, but do you think you looked over at him and there was a person there who you cared for more deeply or there was a conquest lying there when you were finished?

BC: [Pause] I'd have to say neither, you know, neither stronger nor weaker.

NL: Well, uh, put it another way, would you want Troy to know your thoughts?

BC: No.

NL: About him? Why?

BC: Well because he's heterosexual.

DW: Well, even if he was homosexual do you think you'd be proud of your thoughts?

BC: No, I guess not.

DT: All right. So why are you not proud of your thought? Do you think the thought is kind, as you think about him sexually? Do you think you're kind or do you think you're selfish?

BC: [Pause] Uh...probably selfish.

DT: Selfish. So do you think whenever we're selfish we're using the world, and a representative of the world, to be selfish, do you think we'll have to be against ourselves?

BC: [Pause] You said...what?

DT: Do you think whenever we use the world, a representative of the world, and Troy is a representative of the world, right? Do you think whenever we use a representative of the world to be selfish; do you think we have to be against ourselves?

BC: Yes.

DT: That's right. The objection to homosexuality which is one form of selfishness... it's not the only form of selfishness but it is one of the forms of selfishness humanity can go after... whenever we are selfish, we're against ourselves because of an ethical reason. The self is deeply ethical. We're meant to like the world, to be fair to the world, to give, to see meaning in things. And when we don't want to see meaning in the world, but use it for narrow purposes, the whole self will object. And the objection to homosexuality has got nothing to do again with society. We've talked about this before.

BC: Right.

DT: The objection that you feel to homosexuality, Mr. Cangelosi, comes from the best thing in you: ethics. That in you that says you are meant to like the world, the world that made you, and the world that is in you now. I'd like to ask you something else: Did, you study, did you listen to the last consultation? I'll be direct. Did you actually listen to it?

BC: Yes.

DT: Did you like yourself for the way you talked, the way you listened?

BC: Uh, well, I thought I sounded...I didn't think I sound like myself.

DT: In what way?

BC: Well I, um, I guess I thought, when I talk to you, it seems like it's, um...I don't know how to explain it but, I don't sound as much like myself as I think.

DW: Well you're talking about the sound of your voice and Mr. Timmons is talking about how you answered the questions.

BC: [Silence]

DT: As you listened to yourself did you like the way you answered questions and even the way you asked questions?

BC: No.

DT: Did you, do you think the reason you didn't like yourself was because you were really, sincerely trying to see something, or because you were being argumentative for the purpose of not seeing what is true, and in fact thwarting? [Ed.: It is typical of AR teachers to shame people when they demonstrate uncertainty about the teachings.]

BC: Well, I guess, maybe it would be, if I tried to, I guess I would have to say I was disappointed in myself for not catching on quicker.

DT: Yeah, but do you think there was anything argumentative? See a person cannot understand something and they can say, "I don't understand this." When I began to study Aesthetic Realism I wanted to see, but I also made a mistake in wanting to be superior.

BC: So you think I'm trying—

DT: No, I'm talking... I'm talking about myself for the moment. But I had gone through schools and I felt that I, well, had a certain sense of myself, I thought I was fast and clever, uh, bright. And the idea that I did not know Aesthetic Realism and the tremendous knowledge that Eli Siegel had come to... on one hand I was grateful that Aesthetic Realism was so big there was something for me to learn and it was true about me. I was grateful for that. But on the other hand, I made the stupid mistake of resenting the, the size of Aesthetic Realism and the fact that there was something new for me to learn. And do you think anything like that is going on in you?

BC: Yes.

DT: All right. Do you think, do you think you like yourself for the way... do you think you were argumentative in a way in that last consultation?

BC: Yes.

DT: All right. I think you were. And we were ready to... answer questions that you had about Aesthetic Realism. That's our purpose, to teach a person Aesthetic Realism so they can have the lives we've got, and the kind of life Mr. Lynch is writing about, for the people all over Long Island to see... in that review. But, do you think something went on in you that said, "I shouldn't be so grateful. I, Ben Cangelosi, shouldn't be so grateful. I shouldn't show there's something new for me to learn. Let me see if I can very carefully thwart, and instead of answering a question, ask another question on top of it!" You know, the "but if" question. "What about...but if this...what about that?" Do you think you were doing something like that in the last consultation?

90

BC: Well it's possible but I really was having a hard time understanding.

DT: Right, but do you think, when you don't understand something, do you like the idea that there's something new for you to learn, or do you get angry?

BC: I guess I get angry.

DT: Do you think that's smart or do you think it's gonna cause trouble?

BC: Cause trouble.

DT: Right. Because think about it this way: If Aesthetic Realism was something you already knew...your life, you've got a situation in your life you want to change: homosexuality.

BC: Right.

DT: Right. So if other things you know already, other things you've met all these years, had helped you in this field, you wouldn't be homosexual, right?

BC: Right.

DT: So what's your hope? Does your hope lie in Aesthetic Realism being just what you already knew, or Aesthetic Realism being new and big and explaining things you haven't understood, though you've been troubled by them?

BC: I want it to be new and big and explain things.

DT: That's right. Meanwhile, that's the very thing that got you annoyed, right?

BC: Right.

DT: So do you think that you should be the first one that says, "Gentleman, wait a minute, I don't understand this, let me ask you another question if I may," —respectfully, directly. We want to hear questions. But do you think either you'll say, "I don't understand this and I want to, so much..."

BC: All right.

DT: ...or, you're gonna say, to yourself, "Hey, I don't like appearing like I don't know everything around, and who are they to know so much more than me? So I'm gonna act as if I want to understand something, but I'll try to fight them along the way." Do you think either you'll be glad that there's something that there's new for you to learn, and grateful, or are you gonna get angry?

BC: Well, I'm grateful that there's something to learn but I guess, I guess, I don't know. I'm disappointed in myself sometimes if I don't understand it...

DT: Now that sounds noble.

BC: ...as quick as I wanted.

DT: Yeah, that sounds noble, you were disappointed in yourself. But do you think you were just disappointed in yourself, or do you think you wanted to—I'll be direct—do you think you wanted to punish us, because we are the ones teaching you Aesthetic Realism? [Ed.: This guilt trip is typical of the cult's particular approach to milieu control.]

BC: [Silence]

DT: See, what it comes to is this: Do you already respect Aesthetic Realism and Mr. Siegel more than you even thought you would when you called the Aesthetic Realism Foundation the first time?

BC: Well, I'm learning a lot about it, I guess. I guess it's more than I thought it was.

DT: But I used the word respect. Do you think you, Ben Cangelosi, respect Eli Siegel and Aesthetic Realism more than you even thought you would?

BC: [Long pause] Yes.

DT: All right. So is that good news for you? That you've met something that's so big, true, and kind, that it has you feel so hopeful, and therefore you have so much respect? Or is that bad news that you've met something?

BC: Good news.

DT: That's right! But there's Man's deepest desire to respect the world. That's what we're, we're born. We're hoping every minute to have more respect. But there's something else in every person that says, "The hell I'll respect anything! I wanna be superior, even if I'm miserable and disappointed and bored, at least I'll feel there's nothing bigger than me. I'm superior to everything." That comes from contempt in man. And what we're saying is, is when a person has about three or four consultations as you have, they begin to see how big Aesthetic Realism is. And they begin to see that it's true, not just about homosexuality, but about the world as such, people generally. It's true! And either they'll express their gratitude for this, or they'll turn their gratitude into anger. And I feel some of that went on in that consultation, Mr. Cangelosi, and that's why we're being critical of it now, because it was wrong, and it's also hurting you, and we're saying, "Don't make the mistake of resenting the fact that you respect Eli Siegel more and more."

DW: And even this matter about your not seeing things or being slow. Do you think that's the thing you should emphasize?

Because I think that's something that you're talking about again so you don't have to make too much about what you already know. I am sure, Mr. Cangelosi, you are studying these consultations and you're, you're reading The Aesthetic Realism of Eli Siegel and the Change from Homosexuality. You know a tremendous amount. And I think you would be much smarter and for your life if you would talk about that, what you have seen, what you have learned... also what you haven't seen and what you want to see more. But you've heard and you've seen a lot.

NL: Is that true Mr. Cangelosi?

BC: Yes.

NL: Yes. And do you think that long, long before you met the Aesthetic Realism of Eli Siegel you were already very adept at the business of making everything look pretty much the same and as not coming to too much?

BC: Right.

NL: And do you think you built a whole importance to yourself, a whole personality on not finding the world so good, or worthy of very much respect? A world that wouldn't understand you, but a world you still could be superior to?

BC: Okay.

NL: And do you think that in, what you've heard and read yourself and see with your own mind that you do see, do you think you've already had that notion of the world questioned in a way it never has been questioned before? Do you think Aesthetic Realism has given you the feeling that you, Ben Cangelosi, two things: One is likely has been wrong about everything, and two, can really like this world and have an entirely different life? Do you think you've gotten both feelings?

BC: Yes.

NL: So do you think that you are tremendously, tremendously grateful that you met the Aesthetic Realism of Eli Siegel?

BC: Yes.

NL: What would have happened to you? And what we're saying is that desire to have contempt as a means of being important, that has run you all these years, that if you don't want to see it and criticize it yourself and find it a pleasure to do it, because it's like getting mud off of yourself, then there will be difficulty and Aesthetic Realism won't be able to do the good things it can do, and wants to do. [Ed.: In other words, if AR fails to turn Ben Cangelosi straight it's because he wasn't grateful enough. The consultants are setting things up to explain away possible failure down the road.]

DT: After the consultation, two consultations ago, when Mr. Winterbourne wasn't available to give the consultation, and you were told that the consultation couldn't be given that evening, remember that?

BC: Right.

DT: All right. Were you surprised when that happened?

BC: Yeah, a little bit, but I felt, you know, things come up.

DT: A little bit! Ben Cangelosi, you know, you have a way of understating things. Do you think you were a little surprised? I'm, I'm not saying that you weren't understanding, but do you think that you were surprised?

BC: Yeah, I was surprised.

DT: Right, and—

BC: But—

DT: Hold on a second. But do you think as you were surprised, you also wanted to have the consultation?

BC: Well I definitely wanted it.

DT: That's right! Do you think not being able to have that particular consultation...? I believe it was your second consultation, right?

BC: That would have been my third, I think.

DT: Third? So do you think that as you were ready to have the consultation that evening and then suddenly you were informed that due to unexpected occurrences Mr. Winterbourne wasn't available that evening, uh, do you think you were both surprised and simultaneously saw more how much you want to know Aesthetic Realism, want to have consultations? Do you think in a way it forced you to see more about how much Aesthetic Realism already means to you?

BC: Well I have to say I was disappointed but I was.

NL: All right but this—

BC: My very first one I missed because I got the times mixed up, you know, so I was disappointed then already too, you know, because it means a lot to me because you know, you're saying I can change from homosexuality, so it means a lot.

DT: But before you get to... men have changed from homosexuality, that's a fact. [Ed.: No scientific research has been done to demonstrate that this is a "fact."] We're three of the men. That's a fact.

BC: All right.

DT: The point we're making is that, do you think not being able to have that consultation had you feel, "Oh, I wish I could have it." And you know I'm sure you went on and you did whatever.

BC: Yeah, I tried. I asked if we couldn't just, you know the three of us...

DT: Ah ha! That's interesting. So you wanted to have a consultation with two consultants and yourself. All right. So do you think...? Do you see the point I'm making? That not being able to have that one had you see more, that, that something outside of you was good to you and you needed it. Have you gone through life liking the idea of needing what was not you?

BC: No, I didn't.

DT: So do you think this in any way pleased you that you had met something that you care for increasingly? But do you think also it rubbed your ego the wrong way? That in you that said you shouldn't need anything? There's nothing in this world you can count on? "Take care of yourself, Ben Cangelosi, don't count on anything?"

BC: Well, that's very true.

DT: So do you think you got angry afterwards? Because in your next consultation, which was the last one, that's where you were, um, well, in a way being smug and argumentative.

BC: But I think, I think, really, I think that I wasn't understanding the way I wanted to.

DT: All right.

BC: I was being disappointed in myself as much as...

DT: Yeah, but do you think you had a tone? [Ed.: Aesthetic Realists often imagine they hear a disrespectful tone in each other's voices. They attack their peers and consultees for this perceived disrespect.] See it's one thing not to understand, and we're all for explaining a principle.

BC: Right.

DT: And talking about it until you see it yourself. Because you're the one that's got to see how Aesthetic Realism is true.

BC: Right.

DT: This is education. But do you think there was a tone you had, sort of a little annoyed, in that last consultation?

BC: [Silence]

DT: Mr. Lefkowitz would say something and then instead of you answering the question you would say, "What about this?! What about that?!"

BC: Well I guess, like, you're right, you said that I don't, maybe, you know, you're a little scared to believe that something might help me, you know?

NL: Well, but you see...

DW: You see we're saying, Mr. Cangelosi, there's a way to meet something if there's an honest inquiry and an unsureness. And I think you [should] listen to that consultation again in relation to your first consultation and you'll hear a difference. And there was, there was a way of coming back, instead of answering a question or asking, asking a question yourself to be clearer.

DT: You didn't—let's put it this way—you didn't sound just happy in the last consultation. You sounded a little annoyed.

98

BC: Okay.

NL: And it's interesting, this is the fourth consultation. You, you just said it meant a lot to you and it was a disapp... that it was a big disappointment to you. Which means the same that it had meaning for you.

BC: Right.

NL: Do you think you're just comfortable with that?

BC: [Silence]

NL: Do you think that if you were to listen to your last consultation that you would have the, uh, uh, uh, objectively, just to listen for what's there, not because it's you? Do you think you would be hearing a person who was acting as though what he was learning meant a lot to him, and that he'd be so disappointed if he couldn't hear what he heard; or would you hear a person that was pretty much, to use the word—I agree with Mr. Timmons—was argumentative; and what we're saying is there's a difference between not understanding something and there's another thing where a person is already not comfortable with the fact that something means more to them than they expected anything to mean, and so they're angry. So do you think that could be working in you?

BC: It could be.

NL: Yes. And do you think it is?

BC: I don't know. I really don't know. I really, you know, I just...

DT: So why do you think, Mr. Cangelosi, you didn't begin this consultation saying something like this: "Gentlemen, before you begin the consultation I want to tell you how grateful I am to

Aesthetic Realism and to Mr. Siegel, the founder of Aesthetic Realism, that I'm hearing the questions and the principles, and that you're teaching me this knowledge, because I'm seeing it... there's a lot more for me to see. I don't want to pretend that I see everything, hardly, gentlemen! But I'm seeing how Aesthetic Realism is true, and I'm grateful! I've never been happier in my life! I've never had this much hope in my life! So I want to say that as I begin." Why do you—

BC: That's how you felt I should have started out? [Ed.: Yes, Ben, that's how they felt. These are experts at milieu control.]

DT: I'm asking you why do you think you didn't begin saying something like that? Do you think something like that is in Ben Cangelosi?

BC: Yeah, yeah, I do have a lot of hope.

DT: I'm saying... you're saying hope; I'm saying gratitude!

BC: Well, I am very thankful, but...

DT: Yeah?

BC: You know I don't feel like my life has really changed.

DT: Now wait a minute. We're not right? You don't get to high noon without first a dawn.

BC: All right.

DT: Has dawn begun?

BC: Yeah.

DT: That's right, Mr. Cangelosi! Dawn has begun in the life of Ben Cangelosi. Because I know what it's like to begin studying

Aesthetic Realism, and I know what it's like to begin the first weeks and begin to see things new. And you said after your first consultation you hardly wanted to end the consultation because you were telling us how you were thinking about—

[Ed.: DT is briefly cut-off as the cassette is flipped over.]

NL: Okay.

BC: Well, I thought you guys didn't really like talking about things that, you know, weren't in the, you know, what you guys brought up. You know, I thought maybe in that first consultation I went a little, I got off the subject, and it wasn't you know, things [inaudible]...

DT: Things, things what? I didn't hear the last word you said.

BC: It wasn't...I shouldn't have done it.

DT: Oh no! We just...we had to conclude the consultation because there were others.

BC: All right.

DT: You know we weren't, oh no, not at all. We were glad to hear that! It was very important what you said.

BC: All right.

DT: That it's, it's, for you to see your father, for you to begin to change the way you see your father is a tremendous thing, Mr. Cangelosi. Meanwhile, I don't want to, uh, go away from the point I'm making. Do you think you lead with your gratitude, or do you think you keep it under wraps?

BC: I keep it under wraps.

DT: So do you like yourself for that?

BC: No, but—

DT: Okay, hold on! You're, you don't like yourself for that!

BC: Right.

DT: Do you think you'd like yourself more, Mr. Cangelosi, if you did show more your gratitude to the good that has already come to you? Much more good can come to you! But do you think you'd like yourself more if you expressed more of your gratitude?

BC: Yes.

DT: It's in a way it's, it's, I don't wanna... Aesthetic Realism is tremendous but to use a very everyday example, if you're in a store and you hold the door open for somebody, you do someone good, and they just walk through the door without and don't even say a word, do you think you'd feel there was something wrong with that person?

BC: Yes.

DT: And do you think that person would have the kind of emotions he's meant to have?

BC: No.

DT: And do you think he's hurting himself by not expressing gratitude for something as everyday as another person holding the door, doing good in that?

BC: Yes.

DT: That's right. So what we're saying is... good is already coming to you. Express the gratitude for that good; don't keep it under wraps. The next step is to resent good coming to you. And to get angry at it.

BC: But doesn't this here have to do with also that, you know, uh, being affected by the world?

DT: I don't, uh, I don't follow what you're saying.

BC: Well like, like that book you told me to read.

DT: Portrait of a Lady?

BC: Yeah.

DT: Ah-hah.

BC: Well it's, the person, or the uh, heroine of the book is a lady.

DT: Isabel Archer?

DW: Very much affected by the world.

DT: Yeah.

BC: You know, and that's sort of the thing with me, I'm not affected by the world.

DT: You're not?

BC: Well, not to that degree.

DT: So?

BC: So, well, when, you know, people do kind things, or even mean things, it's like it doesn't affect me as much, because I, I dulled it, you know?

DW: Yes, but what we're saying, what we're asking Mr. Cangelosi, and you should really be honest about this... yes, we're sure that you're a person who's dulled the meaning of the world, no man is homosexual who hasn't done that. [Ed.: This presumption is not based on scientific research. It's insulting to queer men.] But, is that changing in Ben Cangelosi?

BC: I hope so. I'm trying to make the change.

NL: But Mr. Cangelosi, even the fact that you can say it, do you think that is already a tremendous accomplishment? Do you think six months ago you saw that the reason your life was so empty was because you, Ben Cangelosi, took meaning away from people and things and the world itself; or did you think you were having the right emotion because the world didn't come to anything?

BC: You're right.

NL: So how grateful should you be? You should say, "Gentlemen, I'm seeing! And the seeing was further in a way I didn't expect through reading that Isabel Archer... That there's a way of seeing that person next to me in the supermarket. And that I'm seeing that there was a way I thought I would be magnificent if I made rubbish out of everyone. And I'm seeing that a little and it's so exciting, because I don't know what it will be, but I know it will be better!"

DT: Mr. Cangelosi, are you ready for more criticism?

BC: Sure.

DT: All right. I think you were being tricky in what you just said.

BC: You said you think I'm being tricky?

DT: That's right. Shocking, isn't it? Shocking, I know, absolutely shocking that we think you were being tricky. For you to say that you don't, you're not deeply affected by things... That's an excuse to be ungrateful. It's saying, "Well I'm not moved by things, therefore—"

BC: Well, you're right.

DT: "...therefore—" Let me finish! It's saying, "...therefore I'm not affected by things, I've got a right to be ungrateful! I've got a right to act as if tomorrow's dawn is meaningless. I've got a right to walk through that door when someone holds it for me and say nothing." It's tricky!

BC: Well you're right, but it's not like I woke up one day and thought—

NL: Mr. Cangelosi! Do you think your whole life would be better if you got rid of the "but's"?

BC: Rid of what?

NL: The word "but?" Do you think you can get rid of it for five minutes?

BC: All right, I'll try it.

DT: Good.

NL: Because do you think every thought you have after the "but" is for the purpose of getting rid of everything you heard before the "but?" So when you're finished nothing will have happened?

BC: Okay.

NL: You've got a "but" for everything and I'm telling you, your "buts" are one of your worst enemies.

BC: Okay.

DT: So what I'd like to do... you're hearing a lot of criticism, meanwhile it's very important because—and Mr. Cangelosi take this seriously—a person either likes the gratitude they have as they study Aesthetic Realism—in studying Aesthetic Realism a person has more and more gratitude. I'm more grateful to Mr. Siegel today than I was two weeks ago. I'm more grateful to Aesthetic Realism now than I was in 19xx with the life I've got. I'm married over five years. I see my wife, every time I see her I just feel she's one of the most beautiful things walking in the doorway. [Ed.: He's divorced now; and he left the group.] And I never thought I would feel that about a woman. Never, never. And that's what I feel every day with the marriage I have. And it's Eli Siegel and his knowledge of Aesthetic Realism that makes that possible. So I am more grateful. Either a person likes being grateful and sees that a life is successful in proportion to how grateful you can be, or a person resents being grateful and says, "I don't want to be grateful to anything in this world outside of me. In fact, I'll resent anything that has the possibility of causing gratitude in me." And a person when he has about three or four consultations—we've seen this many times—they either express their gratitude, gladly, seeing it is as their success, their strength, or they begin to resent Aesthetic Realism, and we're saying, don't make that stupid mistake.

What I'd like to do is read a poem to you, a poem that Eli Siegel wrote. It's about the self, and the relation of the self to the world. Mr. Siegel is not writing this poem about you. Hardly. He's writing this about humanity. I don't think we've read any of Eli Siegel's poetry to you, have we?

BC: No.

DT: All right. So this is one poem that we'd like to read. And it's, the title of the poem that Eli Siegel wrote. And this is, by the way, is from his collection of poetry, Hot Afternoons Have Been in

Montana: Poems by Eli Siegel. And if you don't have this, uh, it's in hardback and paperback. If you don't have this volume of poetry, ah, we would suggest very strongly that you get it, because you'll see more how Eli Siegel thought about people and objects, all kinds of situations of reality. And you'll know more of who he was, the way he thought, the way he saw things in people. So this is one poem from that volume, it's on page sixty-four: Must I Wait All My Life? Or The Misery Song. That's the title. And there's a maxim or subtitle: "Uncouth and not anthem of the particular and general unconscious." And this is the poem:

[Ed.: Most of the poem has been excluded. Only two lines for review have been retained.]

I'm in a deep unhappy ditch, I'm as miserable as sin.

Must I wait all my life, for life just to begin?

DT: So what do you think of that?

BC: Well I think it's the way I feel, a lot of the time.

DT: Well, how many people do you think have said that or something very close to it when they were read that in a consultation?

BC: A lot.

DT: That's right.

NL: Mr. Cangelosi as you heard that poem; do you feel the whole world looking better to you?

BC: Yeah.

NL: Why do you think that is?

BC: Because, um, because I can see that someone else felt the way I do.

DT: That's right.

NL: ...and that who you are, who you've worked to have so removed from the world, is really in the world?

BC: Who is that?

NL: Do you, do you feel less lonely through that poem?

BC: Yes.

NL: Well this is, this is a... are you grateful?

BC: Yes.

NL: And do you think that the same mind that could put those feelings of a person that people have felt into those sentences, into those lines which have music in them, do you think that's a mind that was friendly to your life?

BC: Yes.

NL: And do you think you have felt that pretty much from the beginning as you met Mr. Siegel's thought, either through consultations or more so as you read his words in The Aesthetic Realism of Eli Siegel and the Change from Homosexuality, that here is a mind that was friendly to my life?

BC: Yes.

NL: Are you grateful?

BC: Yes.

NL: Do you want to see and express that gratitude as much as you haven't?

BC: Yes.

NL: Well if you do, consultations will go well and your life will be different. This is what we're saying essentially. That you haven't wanted to. And it's held you back and it's, and it's curtailed the usefulness we could have for you.

DT: So we should conclude the consultation. I respect the answers that you're giving about this poem. Do you think the poem shows a self-suffering because it doesn't like the world?

BC: Yes.

DT: That's right. And when I first heard this poem, it was in an Aesthetic Realism class in 19xx, and a woman was reading it in the class and my jaw nearly dropped open when I heard it. I thought it was beautiful.

BC: Because you felt, you were surprised that somebody else felt that way?

DT: That's right. I could never have described this about myself. I just couldn't put this, what I felt into words like this. It's beautiful, it's beautiful. But this is what I felt. And that Eli Siegel saw this about me and other people, had me feel related to other people who I didn't even know, had me related to humanity. He was writing about humanity, not Dwayne Timmons. But my jaw nearly dropped open that Eli Siegel understood me, and I had never had the good fortune of meeting him directly. And it gave me great hope and I still, I love this poem, I think it's one of the most beautiful things in literature. So again that's in Hot

Afternoons Have Been in Montana: Poems by Eli Siegel, and it's available in hardback and paperback and you should get this. There are other poems here that are beautiful, and is a way of seeing the world that is true poetry in this, in this collection of poems and in other collections, other volumes that Eli Siegel has written. So in concluding, you are still reading Portrait of a Lady?

BC: Right.

DT: All right. Now as an assignment, one assignment I would suggest for Mr. Cangelosi has to do with his mother, the first woman he used to come to a picture of the world and a picture of other women and attitudes to other women—would be for Mr. Cangelosi, if my colleagues are in agreement, to take, uh, two letters, two words from every letter in the encyclopedia, two entries under the "A" section, might be Adriatic and, well— Antigone, I don't know what it will be—and write a sentence for each letter that would have in it each word, Rita Cangelosi, her name, Rita Cangelosi, and that word, Adriatic, for example, to see that she's related to everything in the world. There's nothing in the world that Rita Cangelosi doesn't have some relation to.

BC: So it'll be, uh, two sentences for every letter?

DT: No, one sentence. Take each letter, "A" for example, right? But take two entries under "A"—maybe it's Adriatic, and another word under "A" may be, as I said, Antigone. Or maybe, uh...

DW: Apple.

DT: Apple. It could be something as ordinary as that. And for each of these two words, write one sentence having in it Rita Cangelosi and Adriatic. And then write another sentence having in it Rita Cangelosi and apple. [Ed.: This technique is based on the assumption that a queer man grew up having a limited world-

110

view of his mother—a contributing factor to homosexuality in Siegel's view. Thus, connecting one's mother with seemingly unrelated objects will expand a queer man's mind and help turn him straight. There's no basis in psychology for this technique; and no evidence that it has any abiding impact on sexual orientation.]

BC: All right, so I have fifty-two sentences?

DT: That's right. And there are all kinds of things in the encyclopedia having to do with all kinds of businesses of reality. And that will be the assignment for the purpose that we're indicating, the principle that's involved, that your mother comes from the world, and Rita Cangelosi is related to everything in this world.

BC: All right.

DT: It's very different than the way you've seen her. So, also allow time for the mail. We've also told you about the tape library and you should be using that regularly, and studying tapes of public seminars that are in the tape library.

BC: All right, so who should I ask about like, which ones I should listen to?

DT: Well we gave you one title already.

BC: Yeah, I listened to it and I really enjoyed it. I really liked it.

DT: Good. All right. So, good. So, um, there, we, there is another, uh, seminar title we would recommend you listen to. It is "Mothers..." I believe it is called, "Mothers, Fathers, and Homosexuality."

DW: Yes.

BC: All right.

DT: And that is a seminar that was given, well, maybe a year and a half ago...The librarian will know what, uh, what tape you're referring to with that title, "Mothers, Fathers, and Homosexuality." I believe that is the, pretty much the title of it.

NL: Yes. Yes. Yes.

DT: And, um, also there is going to be a special performance on [date] which you may have gotten the announcement for already, a program called American Ethics, American Song: The Aesthetic Realism of Eli Siegel Explains Both. If it's at all possible for you to come to New York and see that performance, that show, it would be a very useful thing for you to do for your life. So we're not able to talk about that now, meanwhile that will also be in the tape library after the [date] performance. And I was at the first one on [date] and it was just too... It was swell.

NL: Very great.

DT: It was thrilling, thrilling. So we should conclude now. That would be the assignment, and if you wish to make an appointment at this time for another consultation we'll transfer the call to the consultation assistants.

BC: Okay.

DT: All right, so you want us to transfer the call now?

BC: Yeah, and I want you to know I'm really grateful. [Ed.: Clearly, the indoctrination was successful. Temporarily, at least.]

DT: Well.

NL: Good.

DT: We're glad to hear it Mr. Cangelosi, and, uh, keep expressing your gratitude. It's equivalent to liking the world outside of you. And we'll transfer the call.

BC: Thanks.

DT: You're welcome. Goodbye.

NL: Goodbye.

DW: Goodbye.

Appendix Four

AR Deals with a "Bad Apple"

Following, is the transcript of an internal meeting. The author of this book was present. The unfortunate man who was interrogated in the inquisition (involving members of AR's upper echelon) is now dead. His brother has declared online that AR doesn't separate families. The brother, Kevin Randall was present at this meeting. He did not oppose the treatment of his sibling then or later. During the writing of this book, Kevin was offered an opportunity to discuss the treatment of his brother. He did not respond.

The victim, here called Luke Randall, had resumed a queer lifestyle. He was married and apparently unprepared to divorce and live an openly queer life. So he was reduced to anonymous pickups. His AR compatriots found out about it and held this inquisition. Both Luke and his wife Bonnie Randall were, you will see, victims of severe and unrelenting verbal assault.

No concern for Luke or Bonnie is evident. To the contrary, the only concern on display is for the dubious reputation of Siegel and his teachings. No one seems willing or able to face the fact that Luke Randall's resumption of a queer lifestyle provides clear evidence that AR cannot, after all, alter a person's sexual orientation.

You will see that Luke's former friends didn't just want him out of the group. They wanted him out of town—a great way to hide one of AR's more prominent failures. This isn't the only time this has happened. Other followers have been shut out of the group. Another prominent AR leader was escorted by followers to the airport to make sure he got on the plane to return to his European country of origin. Additionally, an alcoholic who'd claimed he "changed from alcoholism" was drummed out of the group after falling off the wagon. A woman who wanted to go public about her longtime affair with Siegel was forced out, along with her husband.

In science, a failure would lead to a revision of assumptions, to a new theory and a new round of tests; or at least to a public admission that the theory is not supported by evidence. AR is not science, disciples' claims to the contrary. Failure cannot be admitted. The result is recriminations and (you will see) hysteria. This is vicious stuff:

Main Interrogator #1: The purpose of this evening, as is the purpose of any meeting of students of Aesthetic Realism, is to see Aesthetic Realism and Mr. Siegel truly, and we have been authorized to serve... the men and women who have changed [from homosexuality] have been authorized to serve as an Ad Hoc Justice Committee for the Aesthetic Realism Foundation to see what would be justice and fairness in a situation, and for us to make a recommendation to the other students of Aesthetic Realism as to what we feel should be as to a particular situation.

And as we begin, one thing I feel very strongly about is the fact that we have a tremendous opportunity to be fair to the greatest knowledge and the greatest person who ever lived [AR founder Eli Siegel], and the opportunity for this also carries with it many benefits to ourselves. One of the things I will say is, I have thought about this a lot, I feel that any person, any man, definitely people who have changed from homosexuality, any man who doesn't want to be completely fair to Eli Siegel and Aesthetic Realism, his change is still incomplete. [Ed.: Note the excuse for failure, here.] He hasn't got everything he came for. He will carry with him the vestiges of that and nurture the vestiges of that which made him homosexual in the first place. [Ed.: At other times they've claimed the change is permanent.] And I think for every person here tonight whatever is talked about, whatever is seen, this should be once and for all every person deciding they want to be completely fair to Eli Siegel and Aesthetic Realism with all the joy and the beauty and the wonder that accompanies it; and I think it is a tremendous opportunity for people really to make up their minds.

One thing I do want to say is, if there is anyone here who feels that they are protecting something in themselves which would have them unable to oppose something in another person, cut it out! Cut it out once and for all.

For the purpose of this evening, we are now an official committee of the Aesthetic Realism Foundation. The request is every person here to see it as your responsibility to be completely honest. That's asked for, it's asked of each person, it's asked of myself, it's asked of Mr. S, it's asked of [Luke Randall] and [Bonnie Randall], it's asked of Mr. D, it's asked of every person here. So first of all as we begin, is it all right if I ask some questions?

116

Luke Randall: Sure.

Main Interrogator #1: We'd like to have facts as clear and straightforward and as accurate as they can be so people can have an opinion. And right from the outset we're not interested in gory details; we're simply interested in establishing some very basic things. The first thing is very straightforward: In the last year, Luke Randall, have you been having H [queer] sex?

Luke Randall: Yes, I have.

Main Interrogator #1: And about how many times? In a way it's a detail, but it can be said.

Luke Randall: Um, maybe about five times.

Main Interrogator #1: Yes?

Male voice: In a discussion I had with Luke Randall on Friday, he told me a dozen times.

Luke Randall: I'll say something about that. I did not say I had sex actually a dozen times; I said that there was excursions maybe ten to twelve times in a year and a half, but I did not actually have sex every time. And I don't feel, I mean, at this point, no one prompted me to say anything. I feel that I'm just saying exactly... there's nothing for me to protect or hide at this point.

Male voice: I agree.

Luke Randall: And no one encouraged me or coaxed me to say anything. I felt it arose from something in myself that—

Main Interrogator #1: [Cutting him off.] Mr. Randall, don't start praising yourself.

Luke Randall: I'm not praising myself.

117

Main Interrogator #1: Yes, you are. So just stop. We're just going to ask some questions; let's just get it straight. Number two: Is one of the nights that this occurred the night that TD and KC said they wanted to be completely fair to Eli Siegel and Aesthetic Realism?

Luke Randall: That I don't think so.

Main Interrogator #1: Was this said to someone?

Luke Randall: I think—

Bonnie Randall: [Cutting him off.] I said it to Mr. R because that's the night that I thought it was. I can't be clear exactly about if that was the night. I thought it was. I know that most times when this has occurred it's been when there's been intensity in Opinion Meetings or in classes. [Ed.: "Intensity" means that one or more individuals were lambasted at these meetings for perceived disrespect to AR and its recently deceased leader.] I know definitely that the night that GT and TR were not there that Luke Randall did go out and go to Washington Square Park and get drugs that night, consciously exploiting the fact that GT and TR were not going to be teaching Aesthetic Realism any more. And I didn't know it then, all of this I didn't know until Friday night when what happened, happened.

Main Interrogator #1: All right, so we're going to ask some questions of you two, okay? And if anybody objects to any of the questions or has questions of their own, ask them. This should be a good mingling of formality and informality. [To Luke Randall] Do you feel that what Bonnie Randall said, though, that on notable evenings in the history of Aesthetic Realism—other times, perhaps—when persons said they wanted to be completely fair, things of this nature went on? [Ed.: Declaring you want to be "completely fair to Eli Siegel and AR" is a near-mystical act that is

118

believed to elevate one to a superior level of ethical achievement and to the heights of emotional ecstasy.]

Luke Randall: No, I don't feel that. Because this happened before the questions of complete fairness came up. It wasn't that suddenly the questions were made conscious and I did something and—

Main Interrogator #1: [Cutting him off.] But since that time, this has also gone on, I'm aware.

Luke Randall: Yes.

Main Interrogator #1: And it also has been up to, close to, and perhaps after the showing of the "Yes, We Have Changed" film. [Ed.: An in-house video claiming that men had gone from queer to straight.]

Luke Randall: Definitely not. There was no sex after. There was one time, not too long ago when I did, being that I work in Rockaway, I stopped off by Reese Park around lunchtime. Nothing happened, but I felt that being in the vicinity, you know, it's an H area, but it also... it's not like if I'm seen there a person would just say, "Well, he's definitely cruising." There are straight couples in that area too. And that—

Main Interrogator #1: [Cutting him off] But your purpose for being there was with your eyes open, right?

Luke Randall: Yes.

Main Interrogator #1: All right. So then the next thing is, Bonnie Randall, you have been aware on a number of occasions that Mr. Randall was not at home at night. Is that true?

Bonnie Randall: Twice.

Main Interrogator #1: All right. Maybe you could just say, since I don't want to be leading... I'm not the best lawyer in the world, and I don't want to lead the witnesses, so...

Bonnie Randall: Well, particularly one night, there was another night, but one night was... I don't know how long ago, maybe three months ago, that it was very late and I was tired. I think it was after a class. I was tired and went to bed, and Luke Randall said that he was not tired and he wanted to stay up and watch television, and he did. And then I woke up just in the middle of the night, the television was on and he wasn't home. And I knew that he had parked the car in a good spot, and I knew it was right down in front of the apartment so when I looked out and the car wasn't there I knew something was going on. And I, by the way, thought that he was out... I had a feeling that he was looking for, you know, H or whatever. I didn't know. I had a thought about it, but I just didn't want to believe that it could be because it had never happened before.

Main Interrogator #1: Why did you think of it?

Bonnie Randall: Why? Because I just felt it was strange because he had a couple of beers, we'd had drinks, and I felt why else would he go out in the middle of the night with the car? Where would he go? That's why. I felt where would he go? There's absolutely no place to go late at night.

Main Interrogator #1: [Sarcastically] Well, some people might go to visit their mother, or, you know...

Bonnie Randall: Not at one o'clock, two o'clock in the morning.

Main Interrogator #1: Or a foreign movie, maybe.

Bonnie Randall: It was very late and then I'd stayed up and I was going to call WS since he was downstairs, but I don't think I did, and then five minutes later, Luke Randall had come home. It was a while later that he had come home, and he started explaining himself, and I slapped him across the face and said that I didn't believe him; I just slapped him. And he was glad, he was glad for that. But that was essentially it, and then I spoke to WS about it the next day. The three of us spoke about it, and Luke Randall did not say that there was anything that went on. But there was, as now, I found out that there was something, but I didn't know then. He said there was nothing that happened; he said nothing happened he just wanted to go for a ride, he couldn't sleep.

Main Interrogator #1: But meanwhile, also it seems that at some occasion, at least, you asked pointedly if this is what had gone on?

Bonnie Randall: Yeah.

Main Interrogator #1: At that time too?

Bonnie Randall: Yeah, I did.

Main Interrogator #1: And is WS the only person you told about this?

Bonnie Randall: Um, the next day?

Main Interrogator #1: Well, in the months following, that you've talked to in the last year about this particular subject.

Bonnie Randall: I think that VK was another. And RA.

Main Interrogator #2: If I could ask a question. You slapped him across the face. I just want to say that I find this disgusting. Absolutely disgusting. And I feel that it's hideous that Mr. Siegel is dead, and the two of you, the lowlifes that you are, would [garbled] this garbage. And I think you're both defending yourselves in various ways right now. You are too, Mrs. Randall.

121

You're not talking straight. You knew more. You had suspicions. You slapped him across the face because you didn't believe him. You had suspicions. You almost let him go on TV. [Ed.: And here's the crux of the matter. The truth of AR's inadequacy must be hidden.]

Bonnie Randall: But I didn't want to believe that he would do something like that. I didn't feel that if anything I thought he would look or something, but I didn't think that he would ever do anything outright.

Main Interrogator #2: [Raising his voice] You suspected he was looking for homosexuality, and he was a man who had changed from H! [Ed.: Changed?] You suspected he was looking for homosexuality. Don't dress it up!

Bonnie Randall: All right.

Male voice: I wanted to ask Mrs. Randall too if at that time were you at all concerned, if you thought that this might be true, about Aesthetic Realism, or were you just thinking of yourself as a woman who a man could turn towards other men from? Were you thinking of the fact that this could harm Aesthetic Realism in this way, or were you just thinking of Bonnie Randall?

Bonnie Randall: I don't think that I was thinking about that, about Aesthetic Realism at the time. This was, it was before the film, and it was a while ago, about three or four months ago, and it wasn't when Luke Randall was public, although he was public in Yes, We Have Changed when he gave his paper. [Ed.: This refers to a public talk in which the author of this book also participated.] Even so—

Main Interrogator #1: [Cutting her off] Mrs. Randall, I think it would be better if you stopped. Miss L?

122

Miss L: One thing: I'm a little sick. But one thing is that I don't much care whether Luke Randall had sex or went out looking for it. It's the same thing. I don't see that there's a substantial difference between his cruising the bars or cruising Reese Park, or cruising wherever he cruised. And you had... if you suspected, you must have seen something. You're not blind; you're married to this man. You saw things. I agree with [Main Interrogator #2], you're protecting each other all over the place. In one sentence, you said, "I suspected," and "I didn't know." Which is it?

Bonnie Randall: Well, I did suspect it, but I didn't want to believe it.

Another female voice: Well, I feel, I'm not a saint myself, and a lot of things I'm not proud of, but this is disgusting. [To Luke Randall] I'm your mother's consultant. I thought about Mr. Siegel, [choking up] and I thought about your mother, one of the most courageous women in America. I love your mother. You are [screams it] DISGUSTING! She could be USEFUL TO EVERY MOTHER IN AMERICA, AND NOW SHE'S SLAUGHTERED IN SOME WAY! [Ed.: Some mothers of "changed" followers were roped into the cult and trained to "teach" other mothers about their alleged roles in turning their sons queer.]

[To Bonnie Randall] And you didn't say anything because you wanted to have contempt, and you wanted to protect yourself, and you didn't want to hear criticism. I know; I've done it. And you had contempt for Mr. Siegel and Aesthetic Realism that he did this.

Main Interrogator #2: [To Luke Randall] I'd like to ask the question how much damage do you think you have done or are capable of doing? You went out various nights; various people saw you, people you're not even aware of saw you and passed you by; you went to areas that are frequented by H [homosexuals].

Luke Randall: I don't know how much.

Main Interrogator #2: You were visible. I mean, you met people and—

Luke Randall: I don't know.

Main Interrogator #2: Well I'm asking!

Luke Randall: It was always fast; it was always late at night; it wasn't in any very public area; it was not like in a bar or anything like that. Um, I don't know.

Main Interrogator #1: Are you interested, Mr. Randall, in the damage you have done?

Luke Randall: Well, that's why I came here.

Main Interrogator #1: Is it a victory or a defeat?

Luke Randall: The damage I have done? It's a horrible defeat. [Murmurs of disbelief] I wouldn't be here if I felt it was a victory.

Male voice: [With concentrated anger] I am sorry, I disagree strongly and I think your tone, both of you, your tone shows otherwise. And I want to ask you, what do you think Jane Brody [Ed.: A New York Times reporter, considered by the cult to be an "enemy"] would give to know this? What would she'd give to know this? Her right arm, maybe? And I'm going to tell you something. That's what you want, and don't kid yourself. That's what you want. You want to go and go and go until somebody discovers you and says, "My God, Aesthetic Realism doesn't amount to anything. Nor does Eli Siegel." And that's your hope. Don't kid yourselves.

Main Interrogator #1: Do you see, first of all... there's, there's, I'm sure people have a very great deal they want to say and they can say it. Do you see that the fact that you've been public about

124

Aesthetic Realism and this has happened is just a death blow to the reputation and mockery of the reputation of every person in this room? And that you hold every one of us up to ridicule? Yes or no.

Luke Randall: I can't say yes or no.

[Many exclamations of disapproval in background]

Main Interrogator #1: We hope that by the end of the evening, you will be saying yes.

Another male voice: Why do you think people are here?

Luke Randall: Because people want to protect something.

Main Interrogator #1: So before... I think everyone here can be expressed this evening, I think it's part of the purpose of the evening. But I told Mr. Randall and Mrs. Randall before they came that they should think what they feel is their recommendation for what justice would be as to this. And I think they should say before people say more, if other people agree with me. If anybody disagrees I would like to know.

[Murmurs of agreement]

I'm finding my way here too. So I think you should say as clearly as you can what, in these hours since we spoke, you feel would be justice in this situation.

Luke Randall: One of the things I thought of was I felt that, I thought to myself that maybe, well, I felt even though I couldn't be sure if someone did, could recognize me from the film, and I know KB said something about the possibility of it being edited, and when I heard that I felt maybe that should be, and I felt... [Ed.: In other words: They decided to hide the facts from the public by editing Luke out of the film.]

Main Interrogator #1: We'll take care of the mess. What do you think would be justice in this situation as to you? As to Mrs. Randall?

Luke Randall: It's very hard to be objective. I don't know.

Main Interrogator #1: I WANT YOU TO SAY WHAT YOU THINK WOULD BE JUSTICE IN THIS SITUATION! YOU WANT EVERYBODY ELSE TO TELL YOU! WE'RE NOT GOING TO.

Luke Randall: [Garbled]

Main Interrogator #1: WELL THEN SAY IT!

Luke Randall: I don't know! I felt, one of the things I felt was that I should not be a consultant-in-training.

Main Interrogator #1: Mm hmm.

Luke Randall: That's one thing that I felt. That was, well one of the main things that I felt.

Main Interrogator #1: Do you have any ideas where you shouldn't be a consultant-in-training?

Luke Randall: What?

Main Interrogator #1: Where.

Luke Randall: What do you mean where I shouldn't be?

Main Interrogator #1: I'm asking. Do you think you should be a non-consultant-in-training in New York City or do you think you should be a non-consultant-in-training elsewhere?

Luke Randall: A non-consultant-in-training in New York City.

Main Interrogator #1: That's your opinion. Mrs. Randall?

Bonnie Randall: I feel I can't bear the idea that the film... well, I know that can be taken care of, but, I guess I'll just answer the question as to what's justice in this situation. Uh, I feel that maybe Luke Randall should not be a consultant-in-training until he proves something different. I worry about how he would use that. Um, I don't think, I think that, you know, I'm just trying to get my thoughts together. I...

Main Interrogator #1: Yes, Miss P?

Miss P: I wanted to ask Mrs. Randall if she sees herself as a victim of circumstance or an active participant in this?

Bonnie Randall: Well, I've been thinking about this because I didn't want to see myself as being a part of this, and I feel that—

Main Interrogator #1: Miss R seems to want to interrupt you.

Miss R: I'd like to know, since you say you didn't see yourself as a part of this, when you got the first hint of a suspicion that there might be H, why didn't you call ten people; why didn't you raise your hand in an Opinion Meeting? Why didn't you make something public, unless you were out to protect your husband so you can have contempt galore for him, contempt for Eli Siegel and Aesthetic Realism and drag everybody through the mud?

Another female voice: Also, you had many opportunities to say something because I know in the last year the two of you have been talked to at least three times intensely at an Opinion Meeting. When a wife slaps her husband it's not just one person you tell. It's big-time. When I did something to [my husband] I wrote a document for the Saturday General Lesson because I wanted Eli Siegel to know. Because either I had to hear criticism or he did. You have to look at why you didn't say anything when he was talked to at an Opinion Meeting about his health. You wanted Aesthetic Realism to be useful to you as to his health, but then you don't say what's going on?!

Bonnie Randall: I think I wanted to protect myself.

Main Interrogator #1: Well, don't just say you think, because it's... it's important. And persons who have information should say so. But I know that you called me some time back and you said that you had been in a team with Mr. Randall and it was over, and all the facts had to be known, and you put him on the phone. And I asked a lot of questions, some of them rather pointed. Everything was denied except for the fact of some drugs taken, right?

Bonnie Randall: Right. [Ed.: Note that drugs seem to be a lesser sin than homosexuality. This is homophobia pure and simple.]

Main Interrogator #1: Not a word was ever said. I asked some questions in this field, did I not?

Bonnie Randall: Yes, and he said "no."

Main Interrogator #1: And nothing was said that there had been any suspicion either.

Bonnie Randall: Right, I wasn't suspicious.

Main Interrogator #1: So, just, it's good for people to know that.

Bonnie Randall: Right, I wasn't suspicious at all; I hadn't been used to... about the drugs I was suspicious but not about H.

Main Interrogator #1: [Cutting her off] Mrs. Randall, what you said a bit ago was that these occasions you had been suspicious were prior to this.

Bonnie Randall: Right.

Male voice: Is this prior to the Yes, We Have Changed program or after? I'm just trying...

Main Interrogator #2: If I could just be clear, in terms of, uh... you are saying five times, Luke Randall, five times you actually had sex. And you went out about a dozen looking for, and that these five times was... when was the last time you went out looking for a man?

Luke Randall: That was the most recent, what I said, Reese Park at lunch a few weeks ago, but before that was the beginning of March or the end of February.

Main Interrogator #2: So you went out a few weeks ago, March and February again was another time?

Luke Randall: Right. But I've always had the thoughts...I never talked about them. I kept them secret thoughts, the H thoughts. [Ed.: In other words, Luke's "change" was bogus from the get-go.]

Main Interrogator #2: I just want to say one thing more in terms of what I know about you. I think you're a loaded gun. I think you're a danger. I think your wife's a danger. We had the monthly meetings you lied your way through. You called me at work and talking with me in a way that... you lied to me in a way that I question your sanity in a way. [Emphasis added.] I do. Something is at fault with your mind, I'll tell you that right now. Because the two ways, I've never... I've heard things about the two ways, I've never seen in a person. And I'm not new to Aesthetic Realism. I've been studying ten years. I have not seen it in any way I've seen it in you. You've talked to me in a way that had Monumental Fooler of the Universe in it. And you said at the last meetings that you were critical of yourself in a phony way, though it seemed to be sincere, red-faced saying that you thought your difficulty was coming from that you thought Mr. Siegel was praised too much and that no one should be praised this much. People should know what that means. You, in effect, took a knife and stuck it in Mr. Siegel's grave when you went out and did this. There was trouble with you in a Time Enough Poetry Class with Mr. Siegel. You were not kind, decent to him then. The way you saw thought was lousy. There was an anger in you about thought, you heard about it, and you heard about it, and your sister, and you've wanted to make less of all you heard about your sister. But I think people should know what you said about Mr. Siegel in the meetings we've had. And, well, I'm obviously going on about this, but I guess the thought that I've got is that you are a danger.

Main Interrogator #1: Sometimes people can get upset when they are honored.

Main Interrogator #2: In terms of that too, I think there is a very good possibility that the reason that woman, that producer, said to you at work that you should talk to Silverstein first, because someone may have called her, I think it's a very good possibility, and said, "That guy, I recognized." It's so unusual for a producer to commit themselves that way about a piece they did to somebody on the phone. It's so unusual. [Ed.: This interrogator worked in television at the time.] There is a good possibility somebody called and said something. Because I've gotten looks this week... Don't give me a face. One guy who saw you on the street recognizing you, just one man, just one. One guy recognizing your face calls up Eyewitness News, calls up Good Morning New York, finds his way to wherever the show is done if he didn't know where it was, and says, "That guy in the tape, they didn't change." One guy does it and then [local news reporter] Judy Licht will feel that the anger in her about Aesthetic Realism and the guilt she's had, and any other press person, is justified and that they are wanting to attack

130

it now and find some shrink who will tear down Aesthetic Realism. You only need one person who will go against Mr. Siegel in terms of the press. Just one person to recognize you. And the way you've been talking about this, you're Jane Brody. You don't need a lot of people calling about it. You just need one. The fact that you and your wife would let you even talk about going on the air! That you would think about going on the air with your mother. I respect your mother so much. That you have a mother so good.

[Loud sounds of agreement from everyone]

Female voice: She said she wanted to be completely fair in her last consultation.

Main Interrogator #2: There are babies, children who aren't even tall enough to stand up on their two feet and you've crippled them for life. You're a barbarian.

Main Interrogator #1: I agree with [Main Interrogator #2]. Part of the agenda for this evening is for us to collectively decide what we're going to do to take care of...

Main Interrogator #2: Another thing people should know is that you deliberately tried in your sloppy, self-loving way to weaken HR yesterday when you told him you envied GT. [Ed.: Somebody who'd recently escaped the cult.] [Gasps of horror] You slob!

Luke Randall: [Inaudible]

Main Interrogator #1: DON'T SAY IT THAT WAY. YOU JUST TRIED TO MAKE [Main Interrogator #2] LOOK LIKE A LIAR! HE'S NOT!

[Apparently, Luke Randall gets up to leave.]

Main Interrogator #1] Sit down! Sit!

Luke Randall: No, I'm not going to. This is crazy. I... [Garbled]

Male voice: LUKE RANDALL, WOULD YOU STOP THINKING OF YOURSELF? WE'RE TALKING ABOUT AESTHETIC REALISM AND ELI SIEGEL!

[Multiple voices all speaking at once]

Female voice: He has no regret!

Another female voice: I hope she leaves him now.

Another female voice: We can take whatever he has to say, he can say it.

Main Interrogator #1: I'll just say one thing. IF YOU HAVE ANYTHING TO SAY, YOU SAY IT IN HERE IN FRONT OF EVERYBODY. AND DON'T STAND OUT HERE IN THE HALLWAY. [Garbled] If you're a man come in here and say it. Otherwise go.

[It sounds as if people may be re-taking their seats.]

Female voice: Make up your minds. Bonnie Randall, make up your mind. Make up your mind! [More sounds of reentry]

Another female voice: [To Luke Randall] Do you think that you owe anything to Eli Siegel and Aesthetic Realism?

Luke Randall: Yes, I do.

Main Interrogator #1: What?

Luke Randall: Uh, that's the thing; I know that, when I do think about my life before I started to study...

132

Main Interrogator #1: Luke Randall, let me just say something.
Let's face facts. Quite frankly, I think you have ruined your life.
Now, you have the choice of either taking care of something
beautiful even though you have damaged yourself, or you're going
to exploit it.

Luke Randall: I don't want to make the double mistake, no.

Main Interrogator #1: So then, would you please see to it that for
the rest of this evening there is one thing on your mind. I don't
think you have much to protect anymore. So would you quit
loving yourself and please see what it would mean to take care of
Aesthetic Realism honestly and truly once and for all? Will you
please do it for each... look into the eyes of each of the men here.
Mr. Randall, you've tried to deal a deathblow to every life in this
room. Some of us, Mr. Randall, have come quite a ways to get
here today. I had a father-in-law who committed suicide this week
because Aesthetic Realism couldn't get to him, because he was
afraid he was homosexual and he didn't think he could live any
more. So please think in that uncharted territory about someone
other than yourself while you're here tonight.

Luke Randall: [Whispering] God.

Main Interrogator #1: So, does anyone else wish... we are in the
process of establishing... Is there anything you would like to say
Mr. S?

Mr. S: [After long silence] Well...

Main Interrogator #1: Have you or have you not been in torment
in the last couple of days, Mr. S?

Main Interrogator #2: I don't know, see, maybe I'm wrong, and I
feel people should say what they feel, but I think that we've got
to... I want to know what Luke Randall was going to do. [To Luke

Randall] I don't know if I can believe you. We have to know what you're going to do, and then we have to decide how can we take care of Mr. Siegel now. How can we take care of our whole lives? How can we take care of the people who need to meet Aesthetic Realism? We've got to find ways to bring Aesthetic Realism to people. Besides that, we've got to make a recommendation to the student body. So there are two things on the agenda.

Male voice: [To Luke Randall] I wanted to ask, uh, ask you what do you intend to do to protect Aesthetic Realism?

Luke Randall: Well, the thing is, I definitely never intend to go near an H bar or dock or anything like that. I, I...

Main Interrogator #1: So you're going to live deprived. What else do you intend to do?

Luke Randall: I don't know; I don't know.

Main Interrogator #1: Well, sir, think! This is what we're here for.

Luke Randall: I really don't know.

Main Interrogator #1: Mr. Randall, I'll just, I'll say it quietly. Which do you think would take better care of Aesthetic Realism, if you came to a decision about something or if you were told what to do?

Luke Randall: If I came to a decision.

Main Interrogator #1: I will not hesitate to tell you what I think you should do, but I think it would be far better for Aesthetic Realism if you made the decision.

Luke Randall: I agree with that.

Main Interrogator #1: So will you please tell us what you think should be.

Luke Randall: I don't know!

Main Interrogator #1: FIND YOUR WAY!

Luke Randall: I, I, it's, this...

Male voice: You want to be told what to do; and then you can have contempt for Aesthetic Realism and work it into this situation where you are hurt.

Luke Randall: I said that one of the worst things I did feel in some way I was looking to be told or asked to leave. Um, and that, but I don't know, other than the fact that I myself decided that I should not be a consultant-in-training, I don't know what else follows. It's something that I've given a lot of my life to Aesthetic Realism. I don't know...

[Many voices angrily express dissention.]

Female voice: You've given to Aesthetic Realism?!

Another female voice: You have given nothing to Aesthetic Realism!

Main Interrogator #1: You've been, as you've studied [garbled] a leech!

Female voice: Luke Randall, I heard Eli Siegel talk about you, and I've watched him in classes at 67 Jane Street [Siegel's apartment house—where he taught] and want to take care of your life. And I... it is un... It's unbelievable, which is what's unfortunate to see you sit there, simply interested in protecting YOUR OWN GOD DAMN NARROW SELF with your wife joining you, AFTER Mr. Siegel is dead, not giving a DAMN what you put anybody through,

135

not caring what you did to every man in this room, every man who is walking around the street homosexual, the possibilities of all the people that saw you. And you are sitting there, COLD, disinterested, like the whole DAMN THING doesn't matter, and your wife is joining you. And then you take a fit because a couple of people are critical of you? [Ed.: Not critical. Abusive.] You better figure out what you think should be!

Main Interrogator #1: As part of the basis of figuring out, I agree with Miss L. I think that it would be good. [With suddenly vehemence] YOU'VE HATED ELI SIEGEL SINCE THE DAY THAT HE DESCRIBED TO YOUR SISTER WHAT YOUR FEELINGS WERE ABOUT HER. And your sister has gone through a very great deal because she didn't want to be honest, but YOU HAVE HATED ELI SIEGEL EVER SINCE THAT DAY because one thing your sister had shown is that she loves him more than she loves you. And you've never forgiven him for it and you still haven't. Mr. W?

Mr. W: I just want to say that I just came from hearing a lesson of Kevin Randall [Luke's brother], where Eli Siegel spoke gorgeously about Luke Randall. And Eli Siegel gave this assignment to Kevin Randall: "It Would Make Me Proud If I Saw My Brother Luke Randall in the Following Manner." Write one thing every day. That's how Eli Siegel saw you. You've given nothing; he's given everything. He's given everything. And I think, Mr. Randall, see, you want us to tell you what to do so you can say for the rest of your life, "I met the most beautiful thing in the world but it couldn't get through to me." And I think... and I think you're looking for the ultimate victory right now. But I want to tell you something. It was magnificent the way I heard Eli Siegel speak about you, just less than an hour ago on a tape.

Female voice: And Mr. Siegel was speaking about you that way a month or two months before he died, at a time when he was in

136

more pain than any pain you've ever come close to in your life. [Ed.: The speaker disregards the fact that Luke Randall suffered from severe and ultimately fatal health issues.] And he's made it possible for you to have a life, even with everything you've done right now, to have some possibility for a life and to live, and I think your silence is horrible. And Bonnie Randall, you ought to say something! Say where you are.

Bonnie Randall: Well, I feel I want to teach Aesthetic Realism. I want to be in classes. I feel I want to be different.

Same female voice: Why should anybody trust you in classes? You have not been taking care of Aesthetic Realism in your mind at least for the last year!

Bonnie Randall: Well, I do feel... I definitely feel I want to use this to be different.

Main Interrogator #1: Mrs. Randall, look, let's make something very clear. In certain ways you don't have a choice. So what do you think, even as to you, would be fair? And what do you see as for yourself as taking care of Aesthetic Realism at this time?

Bonnie Randall: Just as to myself?

Main Interrogator #1: As to yourself.

[Long pause]

Main Interrogator #1: Do you think people have a right to question your sincerity?

Bonnie Randall: Yes.

Main Interrogator #1: So what do you think should be?

Bonnie Randall: Well, I hope that I can say what I feel, and it can be questioned, but I feel I want to do all I can to be a different person through what's been going on. I feel that I haven't been who I hoped to be in the past six, nine months I would say, and I feel I want to be different.

Main Interrogator #2: See the reason why.

Main Interrogator #1: Go ahead.

Main Interrogator #2: In a certain sense, I'm more concerned with your husband ... I'm more concerned with Luke Randall and his threat to Eli Siegel, his threat to every student of Aesthetic Realism, his threat to people across America. What do you think is necessary to protect Aesthetic Realism? You as his wife, you've seen things, there are questions about you, but what should be done now in terms of the film, and him in class, etcetera across the board?

Bonnie Randall: I have thought mostly about that today, and I thought about a lot of things. One thing that I thought about is that Luke Randall and I... I don't know if this is easy to do or if it's not even the best thing, because I do and I know there's something beautiful in Luke Randall and he said he would hate the idea that the film be removed, his section of the film be removed. [Objections from everybody in the room.]

Male voice: I don't care what he would hate.

Bonnie Randall: All right, but I'm just saying—

Same male voice: [Louder] I DON'T CARE WHAT HE WOULD HATE!

Female voice: Stop thinking about yourself.

138

Another male voice: What's going to happen to Aesthetic Realism?

Third male voice: Also, frankly, I think that... I don't know if anybody has just said it out but I definitely think this segment should come out and I don't think there's too much question about it.

[Agreement from others]

Another female voice: WHY DIDN'T HE THINK ABOUT THE FILM? WHY DIDN'T HE THINK ABOUT THE FILM WHEN HE WENT INTO A TRUCK? [To have sex with another man.]

Same male voice: I don't think it's too much of a question.

 [Sounds of agreement]

Fourth male voice: You're not thinking of the people... that people really saw you.

Fifth male voice: It's not real to you; it's not real.

Main Interrogator #2: Bonnie Randall and Luke Randall, I can remember, I saw somebody two weeks ago who I remembered from the bars. And a month before that, I saw somebody who I knew back in my old neighborhood. His life was so different than mine. I saw him looking at guys on the street as I passed him by... and it was something to see in four years, the difference. I remembered. And then, I didn't think about him, but when I saw him, click [snaps fingers] I remembered. And it's everybody here, whether it be a man or a woman, can somebody somewhere, remember the messenger at work, will remember their next-door neighbor when they run into them three years later? [Murmurs of agreement] People, we see them and your memory is jarred. [Ed.: The paranoia here is palpable!] And it's the... well my opinion is,

139

Luke Randall, I feel, my recommendation would be that the way you are speaking, in the way your wife is speaking, I feel you definitely... and [garbled] I should not be the first person saying it. [A chorus of people say he should not say it.]

Main Interrogator #1: Mr. C?

Mr. C: I think Luke Randall should say what you see as your obligation to Eli Siegel, to Aesthetic Realism, to every man who's here who's changed that you want [garbled] to.

[Long pause]

Luke Randall: Well, I don't know what to say at this point.

[Many people speak loudly and intensely all at once.]

Mr. C: YOU HAVE AN OBLIGATION TO EVERYBODY IN THIS ROOM AND TO EVERY PERSON IN THE WORLD! WE REPRESENT MILLIONS OF PEOPLE! I REPRESENT A WHOLE COUNTRY! YOU HAVE TO BE JUST! STOP NOW!

Bonnie Randall [to Luke Randall]: Would you speak?

Luke Randall: I don't know what—

[Several people start yelling.]

Male voice: That's not good enough!

Female voice: YOU CALLED HIM A LIAR BY PUTTING YOUR FACE ON THAT SHOW!

Another male voice: Look at people when you speak.

Luke Randall: I wasn't in my right mind.

Same male voice: [Louder] LOOK AT PEOPLE WHEN YOU SPEAK!

Luke Randall: I wasn't in my mind. [Main Interrogator #2] is right.

Same male voice: Look in someone's eyes and think of their life. Think of me, for example. Do you want me to have someone come and say, "Oh, you say you changed; I don't believe it. I know someone who said he'd changed and he had his name in an ad, and he was in a film. It was bullshit."

Another male voice: Luke, think of FB who came this week and who you spoke to the other night and just left, who is leaving right now on a plane with his wife. Who has three children waiting back home. Who is hopeful as hell. Think of him.

Female voice: I think there could be something from you right now. You were asked what do you owe Eli Siegel? I owe to Eli Siegel my life, my being, every fiber in my body.

Main Interrogator #2: Hear, hear!

[The sentiment is echoed by others.]

Same female voice: I'm proud of that.

Main Interrogator #1: Pretty good fibers, too!

[There's a hubbub of agreement in the background.]

Another female voice: Luke Randall, I think you could begin right now. There hasn't been an honest regret. I'm sitting here; I could weep for years. I have a letter in my purse from a SCUM who said my husband didn't change, and you are backing him up. You could have written this letter. I didn't see the import when I came tonight, but my God, my eyes are open! You and Bonnie Randall,

141

you should say, "I could weep for eternity for what I have done." And it's not just the past year. My God, you were married, you haven't even been married a year. It hasn't been the past year; it's been many, many years. So you can't just see it as being of the moment. It's been something in you for years. But you could start now; you could start right now and be honest, and be humble and people would respect you for that.

[Long silence]

Luke Randall: I...

Bonnie Randall [To Luke Randall]: [Garbled] what SB said? I'm glad for what you said, SB. Luke, you should say something.

Luke Randall: Well, I...

Male voice: [To Bonnie Randall] What about you?

[These words are repeated by many others.]

Main Interrogator #1: What about you? What do you think he should do?

Bonnie Randall: What do I think he should do right now?

Main Interrogator #1: What do you think he should do, period?

Bonnie Randall: I think he should change. I think he should want to see this. He should want to look at what Mr. Siegel said. I feel he is angry with Mr. Siegel. He doesn't like the way Mr. Siegel talked to [his sister].

Main Interrogator #1: OK, Mrs. Randall.

Main Interrogator #2 or another man: I want to know what Bonnie Randall feels will protect Aesthetic Realism and take care of Aesthetic Realism. Quite frankly, I don't care right now about Mr. Randall.

Bonnie Randall: Okay, I feel that Luke Randall, to take care of Aesthetic Realism should not be in classes. I feel that will take care of Aesthetic Realism.

Main Interrogator #2: And? And?

Bonnie Randall: But I don't feel that I should not be there. I feel I want to be there.

Female voice: Why should we trust you? Why?

Bonnie Randall: Why?

Same female voice: Yes, why.

Bonnie Randall: Well, number one, I feel, I feel I have—

Same female voice: Have you been in good faith?! Have you protected Eli Siegel's meaning in your home and Aesthetic Realism and the change [from homosexuality] in everybody?

Bonnie Randall: No.

Another female: I would like to ask—

Previous female voice: It's been a mockery, pardon me, but this has been a mockery.

Main Interrogator #1: Yes, but staying with right now, what's being talked about as to Mr. Randall, you say rather cautiously maybe he shouldn't be in class. Do you think that... what do you feel is necessary to protect Aesthetic Realism? Do you feel that "perhaps Mr. Randall shouldn't be in class" is sufficient, or do you think that it is, well, that perhaps Aesthetic Realism needs further protection?

[Long pause]

Bonnie Randall: I think both. I don't know.

[Voices yelling]

Another female: Bonnie Randall, you be straight and say everything you think should be. You want to be trusted.

Main Interrogator #2: I don't think you're gonna get a straight answer out of the two of them. My recommendation would be, and I'll say this straight, the two of you should be asked to leave; we should talk amongst ourselves. I don't want to waste more time with the two of you. Unless there's anything more you want to add [garbled] I feel the two of you should leave. The student body must decide what to do with respect to a recommendation. If I'm wrong, people should say so.

[Cacophony of people saying he's right]

Female voice: I want to remind that Ellen Reiss [Ed.: Siegel's replacement after his death—she was indoctrinated into the cult from early childhood] had said recently in a class, she said, and I think she used the word accuse, she said this might surprise you, but she said, I accuse you of, you know, letting your husband leave, go to California and acting sad for a while and then joining him. Very sweetly [you answered]: "Oh no." You know. You didn't spill any beans. And I just want to say I agree with [Main Interrogator #2] because the thing I feel is two plus two equals four. I feel there is no regret, because you still don't feel you've made a mistake.

Bonnie Randall: I do!

144

[Sounds of others disagreeing]

I made a mistake!

Female voice: What was your mistake?

Bonnie Randall: One, I did not inform people of my suspicions; I did not talk to people about what I... was going on with us.

Another female voice: [Screeching] YOUR MISTAKE, BONNIE RANDALL WAS THAT YOU WANTED ELI SIEGEL DEAD AGAIN! THAT'S YOUR MISTAKE! AND YOU DON'T CARE ABOUT ANYBODY'S LIFE! ALL THE MEN IN THIS ROOM [the "changed" men] AND ALL THE MEN THAT HAVEN'T BEEN ABLE TO MEET AESTHETIC REALISM! I DON'T GIVE A DAMN ABOUT YOUR HUSBAND FROM ONE POINT OF VIEW. I DON'T GIVE A DAMN ABOUT YOU! WHAT ABOUT ALL THE OTHER PEOPLE? WHAT ABOUT ELI SIEGEL? YOU HAVEN'T SAID ONE WORD ABOUT AESTHETIC REALISM! WHAT DO YOU THINK SHOULD BE TO PROTECT AESTHETIC REALISM AND ELI SIEGEL?! MY GOD I'VE MADE MISTAKES, BUT THEY DESERVE PROTECTION!

[Long pause]

NOT ONE WORD OUT OF EITHER OF YOU?!

[Long pause]

Bonnie Randall: I'm just not sure what to say.

[Same female voices and several others all speak at once]

Main Interrogator #1: I think [Main Interrogator #2] is right.

Another female voice: And don't get a victory now.

145

[Murmurs from others]

Third female voice: You can't possibly get a victory. You are so selfish, that's the thing. I can't believe how selfish you both are! You're so disgustingly selfish!

Fourth female voice: Bonnie, you should go with him. [This indicates that Luke Randall has probably already gotten up to leave or has left.]

Bonnie Randall: I'm sorry [garbled].

Male voice: I want to say something also. Make sure Mr. Randall and Mrs. Randall, as she leaves here, we are trying to protect Aesthetic Realism, the thing that you have been close to in a very public way, which can hurt people. So make sure you are in good faith as you leave. At least the best you can, try to take care of Aesthetic Realism. Okay?

Appendix Five

Resources

For further information on cults and recovery, the following resources may help:

Books:

Lalich, Janja. *Take Back Your Life: Recovering from Cults and Abusive Relationships*

Langone, Michael. *Recovery from Cults: Help for Victims of Psychological and Spiritual Abuse*

Muster, Nori. *Cult Survivors Handbook: How to live in the material world again*

Singer, Margaret. *Cults in Our Midst: The continuing fight against their hidden menace*

Professional organizations:

The International Cultic Studies Association (ICSA) holds conferences and they also offer free articles on their website: http://www.icsahome.com.

In AR's hometown of New York City, the Cult Hotline and Clinic offers family support groups. You can call them at 212-632-4640 or email them at info@cultclinic.org. Their website is: http://www.cultclinic.org.

A Note of Thanks

In writing this book, I have stood on the shoulders of others.

Most important among these is Michael Bluejay who pulled together the website that gives AR survivors a chance to share their cautionary tales. A substantial amount of the information in this book, including the two transcripts, was provided via Michael's website. Additionally, the contacts he provided were invaluable to the research and writing of this book.

Thanks, too, to all the individuals who spoke to me or sent information about their AR experiences. It's tough to admit, especially to yourself, that you once joined a cult and drank the metaphorical Kool Aid. Kudos to all of you for your courage.

Thanks to all of the fierce queer people, the activists, the writers and the straight allies who have spoken out over the years. You are the giants who paved the way for my work and that of others.

Thanks to Bill, my editor, for his clear-eyed advice and guidance.

Thanks to Dr. Bob, the therapist who helped me deprogram from the AR cult.

About the Authors

Hal W. Lanse, PhD, a survivor of Aesthetic Realism, is a writer, lecturer and award winning scholar living in New York City. He's an openly queer man, adoptive parent and grandfather. Dr. Hal is the author of several books including *Read Well, Think Well* and *The Rainbow Curriculum: Teaching Teens about LGBT Issues.*

Michael Bluejay is a former member of Aesthetic Realism. He now works to expose the truth about the group through his website Aesthetic Realism is a Cult. Michael has been quoted about AR in the *Village Voice* and the *Albany Times-Union*. Professionally, he writes and publishes popular informational websites about topics such as personal finance, saving electricity, and bicycle safety. His work has been referenced in the *New York Times, Newsweek, TIME, BusinessWeek* and *WIRED.*

Made in the USA
Monee, IL
23 March 2022

93434101R00083